AN ERA IN
ANGLICAN THEOLOGY

From Gore to Temple

AN ERA IN ANGLICAN THEOLOGY

From Gore to Temple

The Development of Anglican Theology between
Lux Mundi and the Second World War
1889–1939

ARTHUR MICHAEL RAMSEY, D.D.
ARCHBISHOP OF YORK

WIPF & STOCK · Eugene, Oregon

Wipf and Stock Publishers
199 W 8th Ave, Suite 3
Eugene, OR 97401

An Era in Anglican Theology From Gore to Temple
The Development of Anglican Theology Between Lux Mundi and
the Second World War 1889-1939
By Ramsey, Michael
Copyright©1960 by Community of the Resurrection
ISBN 13: 978-1-60608-692-6
Publication date 4/22/2009
Previously published by Charles Scribner's Sons, 1960

CONTENTS

	PREFACE	vii
I	'LUX MUNDI'	1
II	THE INCARNATION, MAN AND NATURE	16
III	THE INCARNATION AND KENOSIS	30
IV	THE DOCTRINE OF THE CROSS	44
V	MODERNISM	60
VI	CREED AND SUBSCRIPTION	77
VII	LIBERAL CATHOLICISM	92
VIII	THE HOLY CATHOLIC CHURCH	111
IX	THE RECOVERY OF THE BIBLE	129
X	WILLIAM TEMPLE	146
XI	EPILOGUE	162

Appendix A. The Influence of Albert Schweitzer 171
„ B. The Fall and Original Sin in Anglican Thought 175
„ C. The Trinity in Anglican Theology 179
„ D. Gore and Rashdall on the Trinity 185
Index of Subjects 189
Index of Names 190

ACKNOWLEDGMENTS

WE are indebted to the following for permission to quote copyright material:

Messrs. Gerald Duckworth & Co Ltd. for an extract from *Philosophy and Religion* by Hastings Rashdall; Messrs. John Murray (Publishers) Ltd. for extracts from the following works of Bishop Gore: *Orders and Unity, The Incarnation of the Son of God* (Bampton Lecture for 1891), *The New Theology and the Old Religion, Dissertations, The Body of Christ* and *Can We Believe?*; The S.P.C.K. for an extract from *Essays Catholic and Critical* by E. G. Selwyn; Mrs. Temple and Messrs. Macmillan & Co Ltd. for extracts from the following works of William Temple: *Thoughts on Some Problems of the Day, The Church Looks Forward, Christus Veritas, Nature, Man and God* and *Doctrine in the Church of England*.

PREFACE

IT is often said that a new era in Anglican thought began with the publication of *Lux Mundi* in 1889, and it is no less certain that this era ended when the Second World War began in 1939. It has been my aim in this series of Hale Lectures to trace the development of Anglican theology in this era, now that twenty years have passed since its conclusion and we are able to see it in perspective. The choice of two illustrious names for the title explains itself. At the beginning of the period Charles Gore was becoming the dominant figure in Anglican theology, and his great influence persisted until his death in 1932. At the end of the period William Temple was at the height of his influence in and beyond the Anglican Churches, and in the double fact of his immense debt to Gore and his difference from him we may find a clue to much which was happening in the movement of Anglican thought. While the book has created the title, the title has in turn been allowed to influence the book in the giving of space to two of the greatest of all Anglican thinkers and teachers.

I have resisted the temptation to carry the story beyond the fifty chosen years, save for a few references to works published between 1939 and Temple's death in 1944. As to the beginning, since Westcott was exerting his wide influence as Bishop of Durham in the last decade of the nineteenth century, the temptation was strong to begin with the work of the great Cambridge trio, Lightfoot, Westcott and Hort. Such a plan would, however, have put the starting point back into the eighteen-seventies or -sixties, and turned the work into a largely Victorian study. But whereas Westcott's last decade was the outcome of the Cambridge school of an earlier period, Gore's early work in those same years was the preamble to trends

Preface

which belonged to the new century. I do not, therefore, doubt that the plan which I have followed has sufficient historical justification, and that the years 1889 to 1939 have for Anglican theology a significant unity.

The reader who wishes to concentrate upon the main story will find it in Chapters I, II, V, VII, IX and X, which correspond substantially with the Lectures delivered upon the Hale foundation. There was first the emergence of the Incarnational theology of the *Lux Mundi* school with its attempted synthesis of tradition and criticism. In contrast there appeared the more radical movement known as Modernism, with its affinities both with Catholic Modernism and Liberalism on the Continent. Modernism evoked from the side of tradition the further development of Liberal Catholicism, first in the later work of Charles Gore upon the reconstruction of belief, and then in the younger school of Liberal Catholic scholars. These developments take us to the nineteen-twenties, after which new forces in Biblical theology invade the theological scene with consequences not yet exhausted. It is against this background of change that the significance of the work of William Temple appears. He gave the greater part of his life to the task of a Christian metaphysic, with the Incarnation as the key to the unity and the rationality of the world; but he lived to acknowledge with the courage of a rare intellectual humility the supersession of a theology of explanation by a theology of redemption. In one sense, Temple ended nearer to Gore than he had become in the middle years of his life (cf. p. 160).

This era was one in which Anglican theology had its own marked characteristics. There was the emphasis upon the Incarnation, the striving after synthesis between theology and contemporary culture which the term 'liberal' broadly denotes, the frequent shift of interest from dogma to apologetics. But if these were the more dated characteristics, there were also the more permanent ones, seldom absent from Anglican divinity in any age: the appeal to Scripture, and the Fathers, the fondness for Nicene categories, the union of doctrine and liturgy, the isolation from continental influences. The gulf

Preface

between this era and the theological trends of today seems often very great. If this era has often been thought of as one of liberalism and pragmatism, these lectures may serve to recall both the underlying orthodoxy and the passion for truth for its own sake which marked some of its figures. In either case, our present differences from it make it the more necessary that we should learn its lessons and not forget its greatest teachers.

In the years which have followed the death of William Temple, the theological scene has greatly changed. Whereas theology is making itself felt within Christendom as a whole, and Anglican scholars play their part, a distinctive Anglican theology is seldom apparent. This is partly due to the far greater interrelation between thought in England and other parts of the world. Yet the times call urgently for the Anglican witness to Scripture, tradition and reason—alike for meeting the problems which Biblical theology is creating, for serving the reintegration of the Church, and for presenting the faith as at once supernatural and related to contemporary man. This witness demands a costly devotion to truth and a conviction that theology is not merely a handmaid to administration, but a prime activity of the Church. It is salutary to study the ways in which this witness was given by the great Anglican teachers in the recent chapter of our history.

The inadequacies in this work may be explained, though I do not ask for them to be excused, by the plea that it is a sketch and not a treatise. Of one omission I am strongly conscious: that, apart from incidental references, I have not dealt with the doctrine of the Eucharist. On this, the literature within the period is considerable, and I have not had time for the full examination of it and the fresh assessment which I believe to be needed. I decided, therefore, to omit the attempt, in order to pass on to other projects of study and writing which I hope to fulfil.

I thank my secretary, Miss D. Kitchingman, for her labours in the typing of my manuscript.

I thank Canon Reginald Cant for reading the work and giving me the benefit of his criticism and advice.

Preface

These Hale Lectures were given at Evanston in October 1959, under the auspices of Seabury-Western Theological Seminary. My grateful thanks are due to the Trustees for honouring me with the invitation to give the lectures, and to Dean and Mrs. Harris for their gracious hospitality to my wife and myself, which made our visit an altogether delightful memory.

MICHAEL EBOR.

Bishopthorpe,
  November 1959.

CHAPTER ONE

'LUX MUNDI'

I

ANGLICAN theology has through the years been written chiefly in universities, in vicarages and (alas, with diminishing frequency) in episcopal residences. In the era which these lectures describe, all three had their part in the study and interpretation of the Christian faith; but the story begins in the University of Oxford in the year 1889.

The academic work of the great Cambridge trio was now ending. Lightfoot died, as Bishop of Durham, in this same year, and Hort died three years later. But Westcott, who succeeded Lightfoot in the see of Durham, exerted a great influence during the eleven years of his episcopate which ended with his death in 1901. In those years he impressed upon the practical consciousness of the Church the social corollaries of the doctrine of the Incarnation. His presentation of that doctrine is summed up in the words, *Christus Consummator*. At one with Hort in the conviction that revelation and discovery were opposite facets of a single reality, Westcott taught that the taking of manhood into God implied the consecration of the entire life of man. The Incarnation is fulfilled in the growing together of every human activity in a unity wherein Christ Himself is completed. The obscurities in Westcott's thought, with its strain of Alexandrine Platonism, were offset by the appeal of his character with its blend of otherworldliness and practicality and by the concrete nature of his social teaching. His old age in the see of Durham was thus the crown and completion of his years of academic work. He lived to see the new century with an optimism drawn from his incarnational theology and his conviction that Christianity and progress went hand in hand together.

'*Lux Mundi*'

The Cambridge school had its superb achievements in New Testament exegesis, in textual criticism and in the historical defence of Christian origins. It had as a result of its virtues little inclination towards the construction of systematic theology; though it had sowed some seeds which systematic theology was to find creative and significant. When an era of conscious doctrinal reconstruction began, the scene was set in Oxford, with the publication in 1889 of '*Lux Mundi*, A series of studies in the Religion of the Incarnation'.

The writers were a group of young teachers of theology who felt a common discipleship towards the Tractarian Movement, and a common desire to grapple with the intellectual questions which Christians were having to face at the time. The writers were indeed reared in the midst of the older tradition. Gore was the first head of the house founded as a memorial to Dr. Pusey. Talbot was the first Warden of Keble College. Paget had been chosen to read one of Pusey's university sermons when the old veteran was laid low by illness. Moberly was the son of a Tractarian Bishop of Salisbury. Holland was a colleague of Church and Liddon at S. Paul's Cathedral. To the last all these men retained convictions which testify to the Tractarian spirit: the sense of the moral significance of every Christian dogma, the feeling for the mysterious in religion and for the unity of sacrament and Incarnation. But newer influences had also been at work. There was the influence upon some of them of T. H. Green, greatly exaggerated in some estimates (as I hope to shew), and yet creating the frame of mind which sees religion as an interpretation of the world as well as the Church. For Holland there was something learned from Stewart Headlam, the slum priest who drew together the sacramentalism of the ritualists and the social message of F. D. Maurice. For Gore there had been the influence of Westcott as of master upon boy at Harrow, shewing how the critical mind and an otherworldly religion can go together. Hence it was that a group of writers in the heart of the Tractarian tradition could provoke their contemporaries by describing their aim in the preface as 'to put the Catholic faith in its right relation to modern intellectual and moral problems',

Evolution

rather than to put those problems into their right relation to the Catholic faith.

The phrase was seized upon as the symptom of a revolutionary tone. Such a tone was already well known in, for instance, the treatment of the nature of revelation by Hort and Westcott. But the novelty lay in the willingness of a group of High Churchmen to treat contemporary secular thought as an ally rather than as an enemy. These writers had no doubt as to the uniqueness and supernatural character of the Incarnation. But they gave an unwonted emphasis to the belief that He who became Incarnate is the Logos who has been at work in the whole created world, in nature and in man, in art and in science, in culture and in progress, and all in such wise that contemporary trends of thought, like evolution or socialism, are not enemies to be fought, but friends who can provide new illuminations of the truth that is in Christ. Illingworth went so far as to say: 'All great teachers, of whatever kind, are vehicles of revelation.'

Rather than summarize the contents of the whole book, I would single out the two cardinal instances of the application of this principle. If it was a principle which seemed new, and might be suspected of smelling of the immanentism in some contemporary thought, it was no less a principle as old as the Greek Fathers. Indeed, the authors were marked both by a contemporary awareness and (especially in the case of Gore) by a grounding in patristic study in the historic Anglican manner. The two conspicuous illustrations of the principle were: (*a*) the conception of evolution, and (*b*) the historical criticism of the Bible.

(*a*) *Evolution* is shewn not to contradict but to enhance the wonder of the divine creation of the world. This was particularly the theme of Aubrey Moore's essay on 'The Christian Doctrine of God'. In the course of an exposition of how God is both transcendent and immanent he says:

> The one absolutely impossible conception of God in the present day, is that which represents Him as an occasional visitor: science had pushed the deist's God farther and farther away, and at the

moment when it seemed as if He would be thrust out altogether, Darwinism appeared, and under the disguise of a foe did the work of a friend. It has conferred upon philosophy and religion an inestimable benefit, by shewing us that we must choose between two alternatives. Either God is everywhere present in nature, or He is nowhere. He cannot be here and not there (*Lux Mundi*, first edition, p. 99).

The theme was taken up by J. R. Illingworth in his essay on 'The Incarnation and Development'. Great scientific discoveries, he says, are not merely new facts to be assimilated, they involve new ways of looking at things. 'Evolution is in the air, it is the category of the age.' But, while it is a new concept, it provides opportunity for a recovery of the cosmical aspect of the Incarnation as held by many of the Fathers. In ancient language the Incarnation is the final act of the divine word who has ordered creation and been life and light to mankind. In modern language 'the Incarnation may be said to have introduced a new species into the world, a Divine man transcending past humanity, as humanity transcended the rest of the animal creation, and communicating His vital energy to subsequent generations of men' (p. 207). Like Moore, Illingworth claims the new discoveries as an ally: 'Our creator will be known to have worked otherwise indeed than we had thought, but in a way quite as conceivable and to the imagination more magnificent' (p. 195).

Thus far historic orthodoxy and evolution were shewn to be no foes to one another. But Illingworth went farther. Bent upon the recovery of the Incarnation as the central principle in theology, he wrote in deprecation of those who gave centrality to the Atonement (pp. 183, 211). This was incautious, inasmuch as the formulation of the doctrine of the Incarnation had sprung, alike in the apostolic age and in the patristic period, from out of the experience of Redemption: the saving act had been the key to the Church's faith in the divine Christ. It was also incautious, inasmuch as it is the doctrine of Atonement which guards the difference between true and false types of immanentism. As it was, Illingworth could write with a naïve optimism about progress in its relation to the Incarnation. 'It is true that secular civilization has co-operated with Christianity to produce the modern world. But secular civilization is, as we have seen, in the Christian view, nothing less than the providential correlative and counterpart of the Incarnation.' 'We can conceive no phase of progress which has not the Incarnation as its guiding star.' These are strong sentiments of the complete harmony of religion and civilization, Incarnation and progress. Subsequent years made this optimism incredible, and brought back the plea that the Cross be given once again the central place which Illingworth deprecated.

(b) The other application of the main principle was *Biblical criticism*, and this was in the hands of Charles Gore in his essay on 'The Holy Spirit and Inspiration'. Gore, to a degree greater than Illingworth, set his theme in the context of historic theology. The essay is full of the ancient fathers. The life-giving work of the Holy Spirit is ever active in the human race: He treats man as a social being who cannot realize himself in isolation; and yet, all the while, He nourishes individuality. He works gradually, moulding intractable human nature to the divine will; and the gradualness of His operation in the world and, no less, in the Church, trains us in patience. It is from the work of the Holy Spirit in the Church that we approach Holy Scripture. Indeed 'it is becoming more difficult to believe in the Bible without believing in the Church'. 'Christianity brings with it a doctrine of the inspiration of Holy Scripture but is not based upon it.' Yet 'to believe in the inspiration of Holy Scripture is to put oneself to school with every part of the Old Testament as of the New'. It is the record of the Spirit at work in the unique redemptive process in Israel. It is a record of history, of what God has done, in and through Israel, from Abraham to Christ. The history is paramount. Yet the writing of it has sometimes included the inspired idealizing of it (e.g., Chronicles). There is also drama (Jonah, Daniel), and myth (Genesis). The truth of inspiration includes more than the truth of historic fact, though all lies within the historical process of redemption.

It is, however, near the end of the essay that the rock of

offence came. How is it possible for criticism to suggest that the story of Jonah is mere parable in face of our Lord's citation of it as history? And how is it possible to query the Davidic authorship of Psalm 110 in face of our Lord's citation of it as Davidic? Gore pleaded that the conclusions of critical scholarship must stand, that our Lord was citing the Jonah story as parable and not as history and that He was arguing with the Pharisees *ad hominem* on their assumption of the Davidic authorship of the Psalm. While our Lord was infallible in what He deliberately revealed concerning God and man, His revelation was given through human nature; and in taking to Himself human nature, He participated in the state of knowledge of His time. He did not anticipate the findings of science or criticism. His knowledge as man was limited. Gore did not develop this argument far. He affirmed this conception of the Kenosis somewhat incidentally in the course of his argument about Biblical inspiration. Old-fashioned readers were shocked that within the limits of a footnote he made this far-reaching statement: 'He never exhibits the omniscience of bare Godhead in the realm of natural knowledge; such as would be required to anticipate the results of modern science and criticism.... Indeed God declares His almighty power most chiefly in His condescension, whereby He "beggared Himself" of Divine prerogatives to put Himself in our place' (p. 360).

None of the other essays was startling as those of Illingworth and Gore were startling. The most original of them is Scott Holland's on 'Faith', which he understands as the response of a man's whole personality to what he finds both in nature and in supernature: God is the Author and Giver of both, and the response in both aspects is the discovery of sonship towards the Father. Aubrey Moore on 'The Doctrine of God' shewed how the Christian doctrine of the Logos steers a course midway between Deism and Pantheism, and how the doctrine of the Trinity illuminates the relation between God and the world. Talbot on 'The Preparation for Christ in History' was a pioneer of work done often in subsequent years with greatly advancing knowledge. R. C. Moberly on 'The Incarnation as the Basis of

Teacher and Inquirer

Dogma' sketched the relation of the Creed to the Gospel and discussed thereby the question of 'kernel' and 'husk'. Arthur Lyttleton on 'The Atonement' gave a not very successful sketch of a doctrine of Christ as Representative rather than as Propitiation. Ottley on 'Ethics' and Campion on 'Politics' were not specially significant for our purpose now. Lock on 'The Church' and Paget on 'The Sacraments' served to link the whole enterprise with its Tractarian background; and the latter in singularly beautiful prose relates the Sacraments to nature, to the Incarnation and to the world to come.

II

There is no need to tell again the story of how *Lux Mundi* grievously shocked the older theological generation, and broke the heart of Liddon, who held that Gore had capitulated to German rationalism. Apart from the specific features in Gore's essay which grieved him, Liddon noted in the book as a whole 'a rationalistic and pelagianising tone'. It is easy to understand what caused that feeling. It was not that *Lux Mundi* was near either to rationalism or to Pelagianism: rather was it that the writers put themselves alongside the standpoint of the contemporary inquirer after truth, and were faintly anticipating the method of William Temple which he described to Ronald Knox in the words: 'I am not asking what Jones will swallow: *I am Jones* asking what there is to eat.' This identification of teacher with inquirer was foreign to the first and second Tractarian generations, and it was in some degree akin to the frame of mind of Hort, who insisted that divine revelation is apprehended by a process akin to discovery without thereby compromising its utter God-givenness. Gore explained to Liddon that his methods had for some time been used by the younger teachers; and Liddon had not realized how far the climate had *already* changed. 'Whatever I have said there', Gore had written in sending Liddon the text of his essay, 'I have said times out of number to people of all classes in difficulties, and have found again and again that it helped them to a firm footing in Catholic faith' (J. O. Johnson, *Life of Henry Parry Liddon*, p. 363).

There was, however, criticism of *Lux Mundi* more well founded and more permanently significant than that which came merely from an anti-critical conservatism. Some of these criticisms can be better assessed in the light of the subsequent trends which *Lux Mundi* created.

(1) There was criticism of the Kenotic theory, produced as it was by Gore in a rather casual manner in the course of the discussion of the inspiration of Scripture. The theory was criticized as being incompatible with our Lord's divine authority as a teacher, as being inconsistent with patristic teaching and as involving metaphysical absurdities. The criticisms need to be discussed in relation to the whole history of kenotic doctrine within Anglican theology and it will be the theme of a subsequent chapter. Meanwhile it is interesting to recall the violent reaction to Gore's teaching in an impassioned passage in the *Ordination Addresses* of Bishop Stubbs of Oxford.[1]

(2) There was also the criticism that *Lux Mundi* blurred the distinction between divine revelation and the knowledge derived from the general intellectual activity of man. This criticism appeared in an able essay entitled 'Theology and Criticism' in the *Church Quarterly Review* for April 1890, the first of a series of criticisms of the writings of Charles Gore which that magazine was to publish. It came to be known that the articles were written by Darwell Stone, then a young man and subsequently to be the Principal of Pusey House and a learned patristic scholar and conservative divine. Stone insisted that in the Bible and the Fathers there is a clear line between what is known from reason and what is known from revelation. But the writers in *Lux Mundi* treated revelation as differing only in degree from the natural man's knowledge of God and blurred the line between the distinctive inspiration of Scripture and the phenomenon of genius in the human race. If this criticism seemed to some at the time to be no more than the voice of an old-fashioned authoritarianism, it now appears to have been prophetic of an issue

[1] W. Stubbs, *Ordination Addresses*, pp. 173–182.

Idealistic Philosophy

increasingly alive in the subsequent decades. It has been asked in recent times whether the liberal Anglicanism, in the period which these chapters have in view, failed to do justice to the unique character of revelation.

(3) The third criticism belongs less to the time when *Lux Mundi* was published than to the subsequent years. It is that in their intense concentration upon the Incarnation as the key to the understanding of the world, these writers and their subsequent followers were minimizing the Cross, the divine judgment and the eschatological element in the Gospel. This criticism was, like the last, anticipated by Stone, who in the article already mentioned was severe about the inadequacy of the essay on the Atonement in *Lux Mundi*. It is a criticism which, since the return to a 'theology of crisis', has often been applied to the general trend of Anglican theology from Westcott and Gore onwards, and a verdict upon its justice must await the conclusion of our story.

These last two criticisms have often been brought together under the charge that the *Lux Mundi* writers were unduly affected by the idealistic philosophy which T. H. Green had made influential in Oxford during the previous decades. What substance lies in this suggestion? Certainly the personal influence of T. H. Green was considerable. Tutor of Balliol from 1866 and Whyte Professor of Moral Philosophy from 1878, Green won adherents to philosophical idealism in controversy with both the empiricism of Hume and the utilitarianism of Mill. Unable himself to accept Christian dogma he helped many towards a religious view of the world. In the words of C. C. J. Webb:

> According to the idealistic school the very existence of art, morality, religion and of science itself, is evidence that reality is something other and more than a concatenation of facts, perceived by the senses or inferred from what is so perceived, and considered alone in abstraction from all reference to the mind for which they constitute a world at all. But if in this way religion is given a place of its own . . . it is for that very reason no longer left in that position of externality, if not of hostility, to secular interests which had been assigned to it by the general tradition of Christendom (Webb, *Religious Thought in England, 1850*, pp. 100–101).

'Lux Mundi'

Green's influence was towards a spiritual interpretation of the world; and consequently towards finding the significance of religion within the world itself. To quote Webb again, idealism 'claimed to be in a position to affirm that the great doctrines of Christianity, of manhood taken into God, of life won by the losing of it in death, and the like, were true not indeed as the record or the anticipation of events miraculous and supernatural in a far distant past, but rather as a statement of the inner significance of man in every age, of the whole history of civilization itself'.[1] If it be held that Green's strength lay less in metaphysics than in social ethics, it is clear that he so presented metaphysics as to make religion and ethics inseparable.

Plainly the writers of *Lux Mundi* owed not a little to the background of Green's teaching. One of them, Henry Scott Holland, was among Green's most ardent pupils, as a series of letters in his biography shews. From Green he learnt much of the range of his interests, and his conviction of the unity of the sacred and the secular. His exposition in *Logic and Life* of the Cross as the principle of the world perhaps owes something to Hegelian thought. But his passionate emphasis upon the doctrine of redemption more and more decisively marked his divergence from idealism. This degree of dependence and difference is perhaps typical of the *Lux Mundi* school as a whole. They are, broadly speaking, akin to Green in their concept of the world as having a 'spiritual' as opposed to a 'materialistic' interpretation, and in their frequent use of the category of 'personality' for the understanding of man's place in the world and God's relation to man. But otherwise it is possible to exaggerate the dependence. If Illingworth was the nearest of the school to idealistic philosophy (and even he drew decisive limits, as we shall see), Gore was the least affected by it. The only occasion where idealism definitely controlled his thinking was in part of his treatment of the doctrine of the Real Presence in *The Body of Christ*.[2] Otherwise, he was again and again to join issue with contemporary immanentism in the name of the living God of the Bible, Creator, Redeemer and Judge.

[1] op. cit., p. 102. [2] Cf. E. L. Mascall, *Corpus Christi*, pp. 152–155.

Men of Synthesis

III

If at the first sight the essayists had seemed to be rebels, it was not long before they became the dominant influence in Anglican divinity. They were men of synthesis, who could enable many to be 'glad because they were at rest'. Here were seen to be united the piety and churchmanship of the Tractarians and the critical spirit which had found clumsy expression a few decades earlier in *Essays and Reviews*. Here was the use of contemporary philosophy and a faith drawn from the Bible and the Fathers. It was an influence upon the general life of the Church no less than upon the course of academic theology. Here was a religion marked by the otherworldly spirit, which soon led to the creation of the Community of the Resurrection, no less than the alert social conscience which created the Christian Social Union. Here, too, was a remarkable group of men, destined to serve their generation in academic study, in prophetic teaching for the people, and in the rule and government of the Church.

It is worth while to recall what the authors of *Lux Mundi* were yet to contribute to theology. Aubrey Moore died prematurely at the age of forty-two in the year after the essays appeared. He was the one member of the group who had a first-hand acquaintance with the natural sciences, and his volume of papers on *Science and the Faith* shews how tragic was his loss. R. C. Moberly became Regius Professor of Pastoral Theology at Oxford, and his books, *Ministerial Priesthood* (1897) and *Atonement and Personality* (1901), are among the most independent and original works of Anglican theology. He died in 1903. J. R. Illingworth remained as Rector of Longworth in Berkshire until his death in 1915, and it was at his Rectory that the *Lux Mundi* group, nicknamed the 'Holy Party', used to meet year after year. His writings, notably *Personality, Human and Divine* (1894), *Divine Immanence* (1898), *Reason and Revelation* (1902), *The Doctrine of the Trinity* (1907), *Divine Transcendence* (1911), were the most philosophical which the group produced, and had a literary grace which made them widely popular. If Illingworth went further than his colleagues in dwelling upon the immanentist principle, a careful reading of his books shews as clearly his adherence to the duality of the natural and the supernatural. R. L. Ottley, who succeeded Moberly in his chair in 1903, wrote a considerable text-book on *The Incarnation* (1896). Francis Paget became Bishop of Oxford (died 1912) and E. S. Talbot became Bishop in succession of Rochester, Southwark and Winchester (died 1934). These two prelates exerted considerable influence on behalf of the *Lux Mundi* type of high-churchmanship in the counsels of the Church, during the primacy of Archbishop Davidson, being more pacific and eirenic in temperament than Charles Gore. If Paget's essential conservatism is seen in his hesitations about the ordination of the young William Temple, Talbot's intrinsic liberalism is seen in Temple's own tribute to him on his retirement in old age: 'I don't think you have ever in any department let the weight of long experience hold down the completely fresh movement of thought in your mind. So if I were asked to name the essentially junior Bishops I should name you first.' [1]

Greatest of all, however, were the two prophets, Henry Scott Holland and Charles Gore. It is beyond the scope of these lectures to tell of Holland's ardent personality, mesmeric preaching, exuberant language, zeal in social reform. Christ Church (1870–1884), S. Paul's Cathedral (1884–1910), and Christ Church again as Regius Professor of Divinity, until his death (1910–1918) were the homes—but England as a whole was the scene—of his unconventional influence; and the Christian Social Union and the magazine *The Commonwealth* were his most characteristic creations. But of him as a theologian it must be said that while his writings were but sermons and occasional pieces (since ill-health hampered him from sustained production) they contain flashes of a theological creativity which amounts to genius. Thus we see him anticipating in the eighteen-eighties Moberly's theme of Christ as the Perfect Penitent,[2] sketching the lines of a comprehensive doctrine of sacrifice which was to be characteristic of several decades later,[3]

---

[1] Gwendolen Stephenson, *Edward Stuart Talbot*, p. 276.
[2] *Creed and Character*, pp. 219–231.   [3] *Logic and Life*, pp. 99–143.

A Free Thinker

hinting at a Christocentric philosophy of the universe with the Cross as the key, shewing in a few pages the unity of justification by faith and the common life of the Church,[1] or in as few pages the inadequacy of the 'Jesus of History' conception.[2] His debt to T. H. Green, to whom no pupil was more devoted, is seen in his grasp of social ethics and in his sense that the Cross and Resurrection are the meaning of the world itself: his total divergence from Green is seen in his hold upon the doctrine of Redemption. His final and greatest service to theology is in his *Lectures on the Fourth Gospel*, where he shews that it is not that the synoptists are plain and simple and the Fourth Gospel an enigma, but that the synoptists are a puzzle to which the Fourth Gospel gives the solution. Moberly used to say of Holland: 'We must never forget that we have a theological genius among us.'

Holland's genius was in lightning flashes, Gore's was steady and massive. In the years which followed *Lux Mundi* he became a great theological power: expounding the Incarnation in his *Bampton Lectures* (1891), his revised Tractarian churchmanship in *The Church and the Ministry* (1888) and *Roman Catholic Claims* (1892), and his eucharistic teaching in *The Body of Christ* (1901). Meanwhile in the pulpit of Westminster Abbey he won for himself a supreme place as an expositor of Holy Scripture in his lectures on Romans and Ephesians and the Sermon on the Mount. There followed (1902–1919) eighteen years in the bishoprics of Worcester, Birmingham and Oxford, when the rôle of innovator was somewhat superseded by the rôle of disciplinarian and defender of the fulness and the proportion of the faith. Finally, an early retirement from office brought twelve last years (1919–1932) filled with an energy as a writer upon the Reconstruction of Belief astonishing in the crowded life of an old man.

The name of Gore will often recur in the chapters which follow, whatever their theme or subject, for his influence was felt throughout forty years of the theological life of the Church. In intellect he was much of a free thinker, who wrestled within himself about every fundamental question. But in temperament he was an autocrat, vehement in his decisions when once he

[1] *Logic and Life*, pp. 102–122. [2] *Creed and Critics*, Ch. i.

had made them, and quick to lay charges of prejudice against those whose conclusions were not his own hard-found ones. Hence a streak of fanaticism limited the liberality of which he had been in his earlier years a pioneer. While he had considerable capacity as a philosopher, he steeped himself chiefly in the prophetic concept of God which he learnt from the Bible, and no Christian teacher has ever held together more firmly the intellectual and the moral, the concern for truth and the passion for righteousness. It fell to Gore to face throughout a lifetime the question which was *Lux Mundi*'s inevitable legacy: if criticism is allowed to modify thus far the presentation of the faith, what if criticism questions the substance of the faith as the Creeds affirm it?

Because both Holland and Gore were prophets, the theology of *Lux Mundi* was brought to bear with overwhelming force upon the social questions of the time. The limits of these chapters are not going to allow any adequate treatment of the social corollaries of theology, but their main direction demands our attention if we are to do justice to the theology itself. It was an outcome of the *Lux Mundi* appeal to the Logos doctrine that both democracy and socialism were held to be expressions of the working of the divine spirit. In the very year of *Lux Mundi* there was founded the Christian Social Union, with Westcott as its President and Gore and Holland as Vice-Presidents of its central branch. Socialism, as both Westcott and Gore used the term, meant the repudiation of *laissez-faire*, and the elimination of gross inequality and injustice by the organizing of society for the common good. Westcott wrote: 'Socialism seeks such an organization of life as shall secure for everyone the most complete development of his powers; individualism seeks primarily the satisfaction of the particular wants of each one in the hope that the pursuit of private interest will in the end secure public welfare.' [1] It was in such a sense that Gore was to use the word 'socialism' when he pleaded to the Pan-Anglican Congress of 1908 that the Church should identify itself with the basic ideas

[1] B. F. Westcott, 'Socialism,' in *The Incarnation and Common Life*, pp. 225–237.

Divine Wisdom

of the Socialist Movement. So, too, he pleaded on behalf of democracy that 'the ideas associated with democracy are of divine origin—liberty, equality and fraternity, real expressions of the divine wisdom for today'. Gore, like Holland, accompanied this creed by passionate outbursts against the injustice of sweating, low wages, bad housing, exploitation and the complacent luxury of the rich. His attacks on injustice were less the expression of a social theory than of the spirit of the Hebrew prophets.

Yet neither socialism nor democracy was safe of itself. Gore was no exponent of optimism or progress. The deep corruption in human nature could bid fair to wreck both socialism and democracy, and it was one of Gore's favourite sayings that 'Christ had a profound contempt for majorities'. Hence he did not, as Temple was later to do, sketch the divine order underlying human institutions, so much as proclaim that the Church must itself live as the society of 'the way', its members disciplined in simplicity and brotherhood, repudiating luxury and exploitation, and shewing the divine community to the world. Where Holland inclined a little more to optimism, Gore felt only pessimism for human society as under scathing divine judgment unless it returned to the righteousness to which the Church must point the way. So far indeed was the new theology of Incarnation from any facile doctrine of progress.

CHAPTER TWO

THE INCARNATION, MAN AND NATURE

I

IT is almost a commonplace that a theology of Incarnation prevailed in Anglican divinity from the last decade of the reign of Queen Victoria until well into the new century. This was due in part to the prophetic teaching of Westcott upon the Incarnation and social progress, and in part to the dogmatic teaching of the *Lux Mundi* school. Of Anglican works on the Incarnation none had a more formative influence than Charles Gore's Bampton Lectures, delivered in 1891, with the title *The Incarnation of the Son of God*. In this book we see what were to be the chief characteristics of Gore's teaching throughout his life, and we see also the opening up of a line of exposition of the Incarnation which was, in the main, to be followed in Anglican theology for many years to come.

In the Bampton Lectures, Gore shews many of his leading ideas. He holds together the ancient patristic dogma and the contemporary interest in the historical life of Jesus. He insists that the Church's dogmatic definitions are negative safeguards of the approach to Jesus in the Scriptures. He presents the Incarnation, in restrained and somewhat imprecise language, as a self-emptying of the Son of God. He draws out the ethical character of the authority of Christ, and finds the kenosis specially congruous with that authority. The Incarnation, above all, is both natural and supernatural in relation to the world. As natural, it is related to process and evolution: as supernatural, it transcends process and evolution, and the miracles which accompany it declare its redemptive significance.

'Christ supernatural, yet natural.' That was the title of the chapter of Gore's Bampton Lectures which was of most im-

The Supernatural Christ

portance for subsequent theological history. Nature represents an order and a unity, and also a progress. 'There is a development from the inorganic to the organic, from the animal to the rational', and this development is a 'progressive revelation of God'. In inorganic nature is seen His immutability, power and wisdom: in organic nature He has shewn that He is alive; in human nature He has given glimpses of His mind and character. 'In Christ not one of those earlier revelations is abrogated, nay they are reaffirmed. But they reach a completion in the fuller exposition of the divine character, the divine personality, the divine love.'

Is Christ then 'supernatural'? Yes: 'the term "supernatural" is relative to what at any particular stage of thought we mean by nature. . . . Moral life is supernatural from the point of view of physical life. . . . In the same sense Christ is supernatural from the point of view of mere man, because in Him the divine Being who had been always at work . . . here assumes humanity, spirit and body, as the instrument through which to exhibit His own personality and character.' Yet all is not to be explained in terms of creation and evolution. The evangelical note breaks in. While Christ is the consummation of nature, He is also its healer and restorer. The world has been violated and wrecked by the rebellion of sin, frustrating the Creator's plan and reducing us to helplessness. Hence, Christus Consummator must needs also be Christus Redemptor, and it is in the unity of these two aspects that Christ's uniqueness in nature and history is seen.

It is here that the significance of miracle appears. 'If we admit on the one hand that the force in nature is the will of a God, who through the whole process of the universe has been working up to a moral production in the character of man, and if we admit on the other hand that there is such a thing as sin in humanity which has disturbed the divine order of the world and made it necessary for God to come forth for the restoration of His own creation . . . we have already admitted by implication the reasonableness of miracle' (p. 44).

A miracle is 'an event in physical nature which makes unmistakably plain the presence and direct action of God working for a moral end. . . . God violates the customary method of His action, He breaks into the common order of events, in order to manifest the real meaning of nature, and make men alive to the true character of the order which their eyes behold' (p. 48). The miracles in the Gospel are thus congruous with God's character, signs of His reign and instruments of His vindication of His own law in a disordered world. The Incarnation is the coming of the New Man, the source and spring of the new humanity.

Such is the way in which Gore bids us think of Christ as natural and supernatural.

> Read the book of nature [he sums up] which is God's book, read specially its later chapters, when moral beings appear upon the scene; you find it a plot without a *dénouement*, a complication without a solution, a first volume which demands a second. Study the Christ. He appears as the second volume of the divine word, in which the threads are being disentangled. The justifying principle emerges, the lines of incident are seen working towards a solution, the whole becomes intelligible and full of hope. But the eye is carried forward, there is a third volume yet expected. It is to contain 'the revelation of the glory', the 'far off divine event to which the whole creation moves' (p. 53).

In Gore's Bampton Lectures we find, doubtless in a somewhat Victorian dress, what were to be the most prominent characteristics of Anglican thought upon the Incarnation for many years to come. The Incarnation was the centre of a theological scheme concerning nature and man, in which Christ is both the climax of nature and history and the supernatural restorer of mankind. It is significant that no small use is made of the current concept of evolution, and that the thesis is congruous with part at least of the view of the world familiar in idealistic philosophy. But it is no less significant that, at the core of the argument, there is the prophetic view of the living God, Creator and Redeemer; and the place of Christ in the cosmic order is understood only in terms of His redemptive work and claim.

II

Gore's Bamptons were the parent of a series of theological works, through the next three or four decades, which shew the connection between the Incarnation and the world-process. In some of these works the idealistic view of the world is half-consciously prominent; in some of them there is the deliberate wish to be rid of the distinction between natural and supernatural, and so to treat the Incarnation as the most significant episode within the general manifestation of God in mankind. To Gore, however, and to the characteristically Anglican writers who were in his line of direct succession, the distinction of natural and supernatural was fundamental; and it went with a revaluation of, but none the less a firm adherence to, belief in miracle and in the doctrine of the two natures of Christ. It is well that we should now see how these two matters were treated in the Anglican orthodoxy of which Gore was the exponent.

(1) As to miracle, it had been the older view that the revelation given in the Scriptures was divinely guaranteed by miracle as well as by prophecy. Point to miracles, and there is the certainty of divine revelation. J. B. Mozley, in his Bampton Lectures, as recently as 1865, had argued that Christianity was superior to Mohammedanism inasmuch as a Christian could claim miracles, whereas a Mohammedan could not—a defect which 'unfits his religion for the acceptance of an enlightened age and people' (J. B. Mozley, *Eight Lectures on Miracles*, p. 31). But this insistence upon a necessary connection between revelation and miracle had historically been against the background of a belief that the whole universe is miraculous, being at every point and at every stage a manifestation of the marvels of God. The classic words of S. Augustine may be recalled:

> Is not the universe itself a miracle, yet visible and of God's making? Nay, all the miracles done in the world are less than the world itself, the heavens and earth and all therein; yet God made them all, and after a manner that man cannot conceive or comprehend. For though these visible miracles of nature be now no

more admired, yet ponder them wisely, and they are more astonishing than the strangest: for man is a greater miracle than all he can work (*De Civitate Dei* X, Ch. xii).

Elsewhere S. Augustine had said, in words often quoted: 'A miracle is contrary not to nature, but to what is known of nature' (fit non contra naturam, sed contra quam est nota natura. *De Civitate Dei* XXI, Ch. viii).

In the course of time theology in the west had tended to put less emphasis upon this wider conception of S. Augustine, and more upon the single point that miracle is the necessary and irrefutable proof of supernatural revelation. Now comes, in contrast, the view that belief in the Incarnation comes first, and that the miracles are credible because they are congruous with it and edifying because they shew forth its purpose. This view, succinctly put forward by Gore in the Bampton Lectures, was expressed more fully by Illingworth in *Divine Immanence*, and it came to be characteristic of modern Anglican doctrine and apologetics. Illingworth could even write: 'If the Incarnation was a fact, and Jesus Christ was what He claimed to be, His miracles, so far from being improbable, will appear the most natural things in the world' (p. 88), making uninhibited use of S. Augustine's distinction between *natura* and *nota natura*. It became the normal procedure not to say that Christ's claim must be true because miracles happened, but to say that when 'on other grounds' the Incarnation has been accepted, then the miracles are seen to be congruous as instruments of its purpose and signs of its meaning. Anglican exegetes have often drawn out impressively the restraint in Christ's use of miracles, their difference from mere portents, their subordination to the presentation of the Kingdom of God in its total claim to the allegiance of men, and their symbolism of spiritual truth, especially in the Fourth Gospel. It has similarly been not seldom pointed out that the Church's belief in the Incarnation was not founded upon the story of the Conception of Christ from a Virgin Mother, but that if Christ is the Incarnate Son of God, then a miraculous birth is congruous with the entrance of a new order of humanity into the world.

The Love of God

The newer view of miracles, however, while it ceased to treat them as evidential portents, brought out perhaps the more vividly that the revelation in Christ is itself inherently miraculous. This has not always been perceived by adherents of the newer view. The answer to the question 'Why do we believe in the divinity of Christ?' has commonly been 'not because of the miracles, but because of His own claims and the impression made upon the apostles'. But that Christ should be one who could make such claims, issuing in a faith in His deity, meant that in Him there had been a unique coming of the supernatural into the world.

To Gore the Incarnation was inherently miraculous, and the miracles accompanying it stood attested by good historical evidence, unless a blind prejudice against the miraculous gave bias to an historian's mind. Miracle was to him the vindication of the freedom of the living God intervening to restore a created world wrecked and disordered by sin. In moving words Gore was wont to speak and write of how hard he found it to believe in the love of God in the face of the tragedies of the world. He could not find that love within the world's natural processes. It was in the transcendental actions of God's freedom, such as the Resurrection, that Gore could feel that God's love was apparent, coming to the rescue. This accounted for the vehemence with which Gore contended for miracle in some of the controversies of his time: it was a doctrine affecting the very roots of his faith.

(2) As to the orthodox formulations concerning the Incarnation, here too Gore combined a considerable change of method with a tenacious adherence to tradition. It is to Scripture that we must go for our knowledge of the Person of Christ. Gore was wont to dwell upon the negative and defensive character of the Definitions of the Oecumenical Councils. 'The dogmas are only limits, negatives which block false lines of development, noticeboards which warn us off false approaches, guiding us down the true road to the figure in the Gospels, and leaving us to contemplate it unimpeded' (Gore, *Bampton Lectures*, p. 108). By excluding in turn the misleading interpretations of Christ made

by Arius, Apollinarius, Nestorius and Eutyches, the Church, with inspired authority, enabled the *plebs Christiana* not to be distracted from Jesus, true God and true man. Gore's quarrel was with those who used the dogmas, not as signposts to Scripture, but as the basis for deductive doctrinal systems. Here he saw the difference between patristic and scholastic theology to lie. 'To Irenaeus, to Origen, to Athanasius, the New Testament is the real pasture-ground of the soul, and the function of the Church is conceived to be to keep men to it. But after a time there comes a change. The dogmas are used as premises of thought. The truth about Christ's person is formed deductively and logically from its dogmas . . . and the figure in the Gospels grows dim in the background' (*Dissertations*, p. 121). Gore was ever concerned lest we lose what the Gospels give us through being 'wiser than what is there written'.

In the first decade of this century the dogmatic formulations of the ancient Church came under severe criticism, on the ground that they tied the Church's faith to an obsolete philosophical system. It was not difficult to shew in reply that in the Nicene Creed the use of a single philosophical term *homoousios* did no more than assert that Christ is as divine as the Father is divine. It was harder to answer the criticism of the Chalcedonian definition of the Person of Christ as being 'in two natures, without confusion, without change, without division, without separation'. A typical criticism was that of H. R. Mackintosh that the definition shews the bankruptcy of the ancient theological modes of thought, according to which 'God and Man are yoked together, not exhibited in the unity of personal life'. Gore, throughout his life, passionately defended the doctrine of the Two Natures. It is important to notice how and why he did so. He rejected any idea that the doctrine could be applied to the narratives of the Gospels in psychological terms, as when the *Tome of Leo* ascribes certain actions of Christ to the divine nature and others to the human nature. But he insisted that the essence of the doctrine was that the One Christ was both divine and human; and was not the one because He was the other, for deity and humanity are not

The Atonement

identical but distinct, as Creator and creature must needs be distinct.[1]

That was for Gore the supreme issue. The difference between Incarnation and immanentism was absolute. Though God is significantly manifested in the created world, though there is the affinity between God and man implied in the creation of man in the divine image, none the less the most saintly men are not in virtue of their saintliness divine, and the creature is not the Creator. It is this which has been for Anglican divinity the supreme significance of the doctrine of the Two Natures. The doctrine attests the paradox of the Incarnation, whereby One who is divine and the Creator humbled Himself to take upon Him the creaturely life of man.

It was for the deliverance of mankind that God so humbled Himself. Though Gore included no treatment of the Atonement within his Bamptons, and gave to the Atonement only a chapter late in the scheme of his book, *Belief in Christ*, he knew Christ only as man's saviour from sin. The Adam story which had long since been dismissed from the realm of credible history remained as the myth telling of mankind's alienation from the righteousness of God, and helplessness apart from the restoration brought by Christ, the New Man and head of a new race. Gore published together two discourses in a pamphlet bearing the title *The Permanent Creed and the Christian Idea of Sin*. The conjunction of the two themes is typical of him. He was convinced that the doctrines of the Creed had an inner unity and coherence, and that this unity and coherence were commonly missed or rejected when the Christian idea of sin was obscured. With this conviction there was linked Gore's 'proximate pessimism', to recall a favourite phrase. Unlike Westcott, Gore would feel that, humanly speaking, the outlook of the world was

---

[1] For criticism of the Doctrine of the Two Natures, see especially H. R. Mackintosh, *Doctrine of the Person of Christ*, pp. 209–215, 292–299. For Gore's defence, see *The Reconstruction of Belief*, pp. 848–863. It is noteworthy that William Temple, in his essay on 'The Divinity of Christ' in *Foundations* (1912), criticized the use of the category of substance as necessarily misleading, and preferred the category of will. But in *Christus Veritas* (1924) he largely retracted the criticism, cf. pp. 126–135.

utterly black. Only those who knew this 'proximate pessimism' grasped the 'ultimate optimism' founded upon the righteousness of God alone.

III

Gore's Bamptons were the first of a series of works on the Incarnation by Anglican theologians who were concerned with the relation between the Incarnation and world-process, and consciously or unconsciously enlarged upon Gore's theme of Christ supernatural and natural.

Of Illingworth's books I have already spoken. They shew to some extent the tone of idealistic philosophy, not least in the use of the words 'spirit' and 'spiritual' in a manner against which Biblical exegesis has come strongly to react. But they conserve the transcendental, not least by a recurring emphasis upon the doctrine of the Trinity as shewing that the world is not necessary to the divine perfection, but depends utterly upon the divine perfection whose attribute is the eternal love of the One in three. This aspect of the doctrine of the Trinity was prominent in the Anglican writers of this era.

The succession of Gore's Bamptons may be seen after the lapse of more than thirty years in the work of William Temple and Lionel Thornton. William Temple's *Christus Veritas* (1924) may not unfairly be said to present Gore's thesis of Christ Natural and Supernatural in a particular philosophical form. Temple sees the Incarnation as the climax of the series: matter, life, mind, spirit, and as the key to the understanding of the world in terms of value. Whereas Gore in the last resort treated the Incarnation as the righting of a world gone astray, Temple (as we shall see in a subsequent chapter) went far in treating the Incarnation as the key to the unity and rationality of a world whose every feature—evil and suffering included—must make sense. Lionel Thornton, of the Community of the Resurrection, issued his great book, *The Incarnate Lord*, in 1928. Thornton's aim is to present the relation of the Incarnation to the world in terms of the 'organic' view of the universe in A. N. Whitehead's

The Incarnation

philosophy, shewing how the latter requires the Incarnation for its validity and coherence, and assists the understanding of the traditional patristic doctrine of the Incarnation. The Incarnation is the climax of the progressive incorporation of the eternal order with the organic series. Christ 'in respect of his manhood stands in the succession of history in the form of concrete individuality, organically united to the human race, and so to the whole organism of creation'. Yet 'the human organism of the Incarnate Lord is taken up on to the level of deity, with its own principle of unity'. Thornton's book is an outstanding, if not unique instance of the employment of a modern philosophical system so as to express the historic faith without distorting it, and to find its own completion in the historic faith.

In all these writers—Illingworth, Temple, Thornton—there is, side by side with the attempt to relate the Incarnation to the evolution of the world, the distinction of natural and supernatural, which for Gore had been crucial. On the other hand, there were those who, rejecting that distinction, virtually equated Incarnation and immanence by postulating a process of Incarnation throughout the history of mankind, with Christ as its climax.[1] Some of these writers will claim our attention in a subsequent chapter on Modernism. I quote now one well-known instance. J. F. Bethune-Baker wrote: 'God is in the process indwelling. The whole universe is not merely the scene of his operation, but a manifestation of Him in all the stages of its evolution. The whole is Incarnation' (*The Way of Modernism*, p. 85). Such a conception, with which Gore and his disciples came to be in vigorous conflict, represents one element in the teaching of *Lux Mundi* divorced from the rest. It is somewhat akin to the idealism of Edward Caird and Pringle Pattison, which left no place for a particular Incarnation at all.

Within the field of Incarnational theology a special place belongs to C. E. Raven. Though the crown of his work appeared

---

[1] A popular instance of this immanentist teaching in the early years of the century was *The New Theology*, by R. J. Campbell, Minister of the City Temple. Gore dealt with this in lectures in Birmingham entitled *The New Theology and the Old Religion* (1908).

in his Gifford Lectures of 1951–1952, delivered and published after his retirement from the Regius Professorship of Divinity in Cambridge, its main lines had appeared in writings within our era, *The Creator Spirit* (1926) and *Jesus and the Gospel of Love* (1931). In a very limited sense a disciple of *Lux Mundi*, and more properly a disciple of Hort, Raven (himself an ardent student of botany and ornithology, as well as of the history of the natural sciences) used to lament that Gore, having affirmed the importance of nature, was insufficiently interested in it, and treated it merely as the stage and scenery of a drama of God and fallen humanity. Raven saw the greatest significance for Christian thought in the decline of the mechanistic biology which had been common in the post-Darwinian era, and in the possibilities of the concept of 'emergent evolution' expounded in Lloyd-Morgan's Gifford Lectures on *Life, Mind and Spirit*. In the emerging universe God discloses Himself everywhere and always, but in varying degrees of significance. In this process of the growing divine self-disclosure and the growing unity of God and Man, Jesus has a unique place, for which the Nicene definition of His Person is the due expression. But it is a process in which creation and redemption are one and the same thing, and the distinction of nature and supernature has no validity. Throughout the process there is a law of living through dying to which the Cross and Resurrection of Christ is the climax and the key.[1]

Raven's work was, in effect, a development of one aspect of the *Lux Mundi* doctrine with the rejection of the other. The main line of succession from Gore and Illingworth ran rather to Temple and Thornton. To them, the affinity of God and Man, created in the divine image, and the work of the Logos in nature and history did not prevent a particularity in the Biblical revelation and a distinction of supernatural and natural as essential parts of the doctrinal scheme. But if Raven's thesis be rejected, and the distinction of natural and supernatural be retained, there remains a task of synthesis which *Lux Mundi* had initiated but hardly completed.

[1] I have written a fuller appreciation of Raven's work in my *Durham Essays and Addresses*, pp. 35–40.

Unity and Meaning

IV

Modern Anglican theology owes many of its characteristics to the central place held within it by the Incarnation. Anglicanism has, for instance, dwelt much on the Nicene and Chalcedonian dogmas and on those ancient Fathers who directly interpreted them. Always somewhat insular in its attitude to continental theology, Anglicanism in these years paid little heed to continental movements and writers, except when they concerned the Person of Christ, in history or dogma: as did the writings of Harnack, Ritschl and Schweitzer. Furthermore, the doctrine of the Incarnate Christ as the Logos gave a constant impulse towards relating the Incarnation, wherever possible, with contemporary movements in thought or social progress.

The question is now being asked in retrospect: is there an inevitable loss in theological perspective or proportion if the Incarnation is allowed to become the centre of theology?

It must once more be insisted that the theology of Gore and his disciples was emphatically a theology of redemption. The Incarnation was effectual only because the Incarnate died and rose again, and the very mode and manner of the Incarnation were determined by its redemptive character. None the less, when the Incarnation is made the centre it easily follows that: (i) *explanation* rather than *atonement* can tend to dominate the theological scene, (ii) that *reason* can depress the place and meaning of *faith* in the approach to revealed truth, (iii) that the giving of prominence to this particular dogma can cause other categories of Biblical language and thought to recede from their rightful prominence. These weaknesses have been alleged in the long-term effects of the Anglican incarnational theology.

There is some truth in the allegations.

(1) With the Incarnation as its centre, theology can cause its adherents to cherish it as a means of explaining the world, as if to say: 'Thanks to the Incarnation, nature and man make sense, and the world has unity and meaning.' That is indeed a

proper rôle for theology to have. But it proved possible for philosophical theologians so to pursue it as to travel far from the sort of faith which, seeing no hope for a world sin-racked and frustrated, throws itself empty on the Cross of Christ and knows that the world *cannot* be explained until it has been radically changed. We shall see in a later lecture how William Temple, after pursuing a theology of explanation over many of its pitfalls, came to confess that the needs of the hour bade a theology of explanation yield place to a theology of redemption.

(2) Again, with the Incarnation as its centre, the concept of revelation easily becomes somewhat intellectualized by a sort of rationalism. Such rationalism may appear in a tendency to speak as if we moved progressively from discerning God in nature to discerning Him in man, and thence to discerning Him in Christ—whereas it may be that it is only through knowing God in Christ that we are able to believe in Him in relation to nature and man.

(3) Again, may not the use of the Incarnation as the central principle go hand in hand with a soft-pedalling of other Biblical categories? There have been occasions when the Anglican divinity of our period assumed the Incarnation as the basis, and thence passed on to various non-Biblical categories for its exposition. This is a process amply justified in the work of interpretation. But there is the danger that while the Bible serves as the ground and base of theology it is not quite allowed to tell its own tale in its own way. The Bible contains theological themes which 'Incarnation' alone does not convey.

These gravamina, therefore, have cause. But they are rightly seen only alongside what the Anglican theology of Incarnation was achieving. It enabled a genuine contact between supernatural religion and contemporary culture. It enabled a meeting-place between revelation and the keen contemporary sense of the importance of historical inquiry. In the hands of such an exponent as Charles Gore it was impregnated with the conviction that Christ is known only as the restorer of a sinful race, and that divine truth is known only by those who will stand

The Word-made-Flesh

under the divine judgment. Furthermore, it enabled modern Anglicanism to face many modern tasks with its roots still in the Fathers of the ancient Church; and it conserved in modern Anglicanism that sense of the creature's adoration of the Creator which the doctrine of the Word-made-Flesh keeps ever at the heart of religion.

CHAPTER THREE

THE INCARNATION AND KENOSIS

I

THE doctrine of the kenosis of the Son of God appeared in Gore's essay in *Lux Mundi* somewhat incidentally, being there discussed not for its own sake, but for its bearing upon the belief in the inerrancy of the Old Testament. Subsequently, Gore and others drew out the doctrine of kenosis and its implications, and through their influence it came to be prominent in Anglican theology. But to understand its place in Anglican theology it is necessary to step back a little and see it in the wider perspective of ancient and modern thought.

The word 'kenosis' is derived as a theological term from Philippians 2: 5–11. In that passage S. Paul is urging the duty of humility in the Christian life, and he appeals to the humility of our Lord 'who being in the form [morphē] of God did not count it a thing to be snatched [or grasped] to be equal with God, but emptied himself, taking the form [morphē] of a slave; and being found in the likeness of men he humbled himself even unto death, yea the death of the Cross'. The passage describes the act of humility whereby the Son of God became man in the Incarnation: an act before and behind the humiliation of suffering and death upon earth. It is, however, very precarious to find exact metaphysics in this passage, as if it defined the self-emptying in terms of an abnegation of this or that attribute or prerogative. Rather does the force of the passage seem to be that the Son of God, possessing the essence of deity, did not regard this as to be grasped at for his own enjoyment, but made it the occasion of an act of self-sacrifice towards mankind. His deity, in other words, issued in generous self-giving, not in self-aggrandizement. But the verb 'he emptied himself' has no

Kenotic Doctrine

second object, as if to define that of which He emptied Himself. He emptied Himself, as one pouring himself out (cf. the use of the verb in 2 Cor. 8: 9).

This passage, however, is not the real source of what is called kenotic doctrine. That doctrine has sprung from the consideration of the historical data of our Lord's life considered side by side with the belief in His deity. On the one hand, the Gospels depict Jesus Christ as living a genuinely human life: He advances in knowledge, He learns, He asks questions as needing to know the answer, He shews ignorance (cf. Mark 13: 32). On the other hand, the Church worships Him as divine, and reads in the Gospels of His perfect revelation of the Father. How were Christian teachers to express the two aspects of the Incarnation, without allowing the one to override the other? It was one thing to assert the dogma of perfect Godhead and perfect Manhood co-existing in the one Person. What was more difficult was to teach about the Incarnate life without making the humanity seem unreal or the deity seem to be ousted by the human limitations. Inevitably the problem came to be more keenly felt in the modern Church with its concern for history than it had been in the ancient Church with its concentration upon the framework of dogmatic definition.

The problem had, however, been felt within the ancient Church. One type of teaching was that the divine Son caused His divine powers to be 'quiescent', so that the actions or sufferings proper to manhood were not made unreal by manifestation of divine power. Thus Irenaeus wrote of 'the Logos being quiescent [literally "sleeping"] during the temptation, the crucifixion and the death: but being associated with the manhood in the victory, the endurance and the resurrection' (*Adv. Haer.* iii, 11. 3). Another type of teaching dismissed any notion of a 'quiescence' of the divine Word, since the Word is 'unlimited': but held that on each occasion in the Incarnate life the divine Word willed to permit human experiences to prevail over Him. Thus Cyril of Alexandria said 'he granted to the measures of the manhood the rule over himself' (*Quod unus sit Christus*, viii, 1, 319). These theories which contrived to do justice to the real manhood of Jesus were, however, whatever their value, rendered nugatory by the exegesis of the crucial passages. Thus it was the frequent habit of patristic writers to explain away Christ's professed ignorance of the date of the Parousia in Mark 13: 32 as a pretended ignorance. A belief in the dogma of Christ's humanity was thus all too often accompanied by exegesis which contradicted it. Scholastic theology went further, and by *a priori* theories of the effect of the deity upon the humanity presented a picture of our Lord far removed from the facts recorded in Scripture.[1]

Now in the modern Church the greater interest in the historic portrait of Jesus required not only that the dogma of His perfect manhood be affirmed, but also that practical exegesis should do full justice to that manhood. The issue of which many modern theologians have been conscious was put thus by Gore himself: 'Nor will it suffice to say that the Son was limited in knowledge in respect of his manhood, so long as we so juxtaposit the omniscient Godhead with the limited manhood as to destroy the impression that He, the Christ, the Son of God, was *personally* living, praying, thinking, speaking and acting—even working miracles—under the limitations of manhood' (*Dissertations*, p. 203). What is the answer? It was possible to cut the knot by adopting a doctrine of an adoptionist, Nestorian or exclusively symbolic kind. Or it was possible to retain the ancient doctrine and to draw out, in a way that the ancient Church had never done, the conception of the self-emptying.

There were first the kenotic theories to which the adjectives 'classic', 'extreme', 'full-blooded' are appropriate. These were theories advanced by Lutheran theologians such as Thomasius (*Christi Person und Werk*, 1853–1855), and Godet (*Gospel of S. John*, English trans.), that at the Incarnation the divine Logos 'depotentiated' himself by abandoning divine attributes altogether. It is hard to see how this conception is not pure mythology, or how Deity's attributes can be separated from Deity; or how, if the attributes are so abandoned, Deity is revealed in the Incarnation. More impression was made by a rather different

[1] Cf. illustrations in Gore, *Dissertations*, pp. 166–178.

Christian Theism

theory of Dörner (*Doctrine of the Person of Christ*, English trans., 1861) that the Incarnation was a gradual process whereby the Deity was restrained and the Humanity grew in the one Christ —a theory in which it is not hard to recognize Hegelian influence. In England the only theologian to present a theory resembling the continental kenoticists was A. M. Fairbairn, the Congregational divine, who used a distinction between 'physical' and 'ethical' attributes of Deity.[1] None of these theories endured, in face of the obvious criticisms of them. They were indeed no more than a rather remote background to the far more cautious and less speculative use of the kenotic principle in English theology. Charles Wesley could write with the licence of rhetoric:

> He left His Father's home above,
> So free, so infinite His grace,
> *Emptied Himself of all but love,*
> And bled for Adam's helpless race.

But is not the unity of Love and Omnipotence of the very essence of Christian theism?

To the continental doctrines of kenosis it would seem that Gore owed very little. Indeed, it is probable that his own thought on the subject developed quite independently of them; though he included an account and criticism of them in his fullest discussion, the essay on 'The Consciousness of our Lord' in the volume of *Dissertations* (1895). It is to that essay that we look to study Gore's kenotic teaching, as well as to the briefer treatment in his Bampton Lectures and the later recapitulation in *Belief in Christ* (1921).

Gore reacted with horror from the idea stated in Liddon's Bampton Lectures that 'the knowledge infused into the human soul of Jesus was ordinarily and practically equivalent to omniscience'.[2] His care was to safeguard what he believed to be the Gospel picture of Christ's real humanity, and therefore 'it was necessary that He should be without the exercise of such

[1] A. M. Fairbairn, *Christ in Modern Theology*, pp. 470–478.
[2] H. P. Liddon, *The Divinity of our Lord and Saviour Jesus Christ*, fourteenth edition, p. 474.

The Incarnation and Kenosis

divine prerogatives as would have made His human experience impossible'. But how did this happen? Gore used the word 'abandonment'. In several passages in the Bampton Lectures he wrote of the 'abandonment' by Christ of certain divine 'prerogatives'—a somewhat vague and rhetorical word. Once only he wrote of an abandonment of divine 'attributes', and that was in a passage which he was subsequently to modify.[1] In his most mature exposition of his thought, in *Belief in Christ* (p. 225), Gore said no more than that 'He emptied Himself of divine prerogatives so far as was involved in becoming man, and growing, feeling, thinking and suffering as a Man'. The question arises whether the self-emptying was a continual refusal to exercise the divine consciousness (a view not so very far from some phrases in the ancient Fathers), or whether it was once for all involved in the act whereby the Son of God entered into the limiting conditions of manhood. Gore was aware that he had not answered the question: 'I think if we are wise, we shall not attempt to answer the question. We have not the knowledge of the inner life of Jesus which would make an answer possible' (p. 226).

The upshot of this is that what was vital for Gore was not the assertion of a metaphysical theory so much as the assertion of the historical fact of Christ's human limitations, and of the necessity of *some* view of the operation of the divine consciousness, which does not imply that it overrides them. He was sure that this involved *some sort* of kenosis, and he had no difficulty in believing that some sort of kenosis was congruous with the divine method of dealing with the finite world of nature and history. 'All real sympathy of the unconditioned for the conditioned demands, so far as we can see, the power of self-limitation.' 'The method of God in history, like the method of God in nature, is to an astonishing degree self-restraining.' 'It

---

[1] The passage is in *Dissertations*, p. 206. In the first edition Gore wrote: 'a real abandonment of divine prerogatives and attributes by the Eternal Son within a certain sphere'. This was altered in the second edition to: 'real abandonment of the exercise of divine prerogatives . . .' This alteration suggests that Gore was ill at ease with the metaphysical aspect of his doctrine.

Unity of God and Man

is physical power which makes itself felt only in self-assertion and pressure: it is the higher power of love which is shewn in self-effacement' (*Bampton Lectures*, p. 160). It was this moral appeal of the kenotic principle which was very congenial to Gore. It is hard to doubt that he would have been familiar with the words of Gregory of Nyssa 'that the omnipotence of the divine nature should have strength to descend to the lowliness of humanity furnishes a more manifest proof of power than even the greatness of the miracles ... the sublimity is seen in lowliness, and yet the loftiness descends not' (*Oratio Catechetica Magna*, XXIV).

It fell to subsequent kenotic writers to fill the gaps which Gore had left. In the light of history, it has seemed that, while he was blazing a trail for a very new type of teaching, his own position was not as far as at first appeared from the older orthodox standpoint of Liddon and Bright.[1] This may be the best point for us to note the criticism of Gore and other kenotic writers made by E. L. Mascall in his *Christ, the Christian and the Church* (1946). He criticizes them for trying to solve Christological questions in terms of psychology, and for creating their theory on account of a psychological approach. If this is true of some of the kenotic writers, such as Sanday, who deliberately employed a psychological concept ('the subconscious') to assist the understanding of the unity of God and Man in Christ,[2] it is utterly untrue of Gore, whose motive from first to last was a concern for the historical data. But Mascall also criticizes them for thinking of the Incarnation too much as the retraction of Deity to the restraint of manhood, rather than as the assumption of manhood and its enhancement as the most fitting instrument of Deity—'the taking of manhood into God'. This is fair criticism: and a reminder of an aspect of the doctrine of the Incarnation which is needed to balance that aspect upon which the kenotic writers were concentrating. I do not, however, think it abolishes the problem with which they were dealing, nor the fitness of their attempting to deal with it.

---

[1] Cf. W. Bright, *Waymarks in Church History*, Appendix G.

[2] W. Sanday, *Christology and Personality*, 1910: a psychological study which proved to be of no more than passing interest.

II

'This kenotic theory is taken up by many almost as *pax vobiscum* was by a personage in Ivanhoe.'[1] So wrote William Bright, alarmed at what he felt to be a stampede of all and sundry after the kenotic doctrine. In the twenty years from 1890 to 1910 the subject had a prominence such as it has never had in English theology before or since. Perhaps there was something in the Anglican climate which created for it this prominence: the propensity both for patristic orthodoxy and for Gospel criticism, the emphasis upon the Incarnation even more than upon the Cross as the primary scene of redemptive love, and the tendency to interpret the ancient term 'Person' or 'Hypostasis' in a sense which approximated to 'Person' in the modern usage. There came about a tendency to think of the problems of the Incarnation in terms of 'consciousness', not through any strictly psychological motive but through the influences which we have mentioned.

The first thorough treatment of kenosis in relation to the consciousness of our Lord was made by Frank Weston in *The One Christ* (1907). Weston was Canon and Chancellor of Zanzibar Cathedral, and he was to become in later years Bishop of Zanzibar and a leader of the more extreme wing of the Anglo-Catholics. In this book he writes with an eye both to Alexandrine orthodoxy and to the study of the human figure of Jesus in the Gospels. He held it to be no disloyalty to the ancient doctrine of the unchangeable person of the One Divine Word who took human nature upon Himself, to question the mode in which the Fathers thought of the unity of God and Man in Christ. Thus, in Cyril of Alexandria's teaching, the reality of the manhood is obscured, since the human experiences of Christ are made possible only by an act of restraint on each occasion by the divine Word; and, therefore, 'the human nature can never adequately mediate the self-expression of the Eternal Son'. But while Weston finds patristic teaching inadequate on this score he keeps his severest strictures for the extreme kenotic

[1] *Selected Letters of William Bright*, edited by B. J. Kidd, p. 34.

Divine Sonship

doctrine of the 'self-abandoned Logos', adding to the familiar criticisms yet one more criticism which perhaps an Anglican would be specially alert to make—that if the divine glory were abandoned during the Incarnate life, we seem to be robbed of the glorifying of the human nature in Christ with the Ascension as its climax.

What then? If the human experiences of Christ were real, it could not be by the divine Word retaining the powers of deity and occasionally restricting them or making them quiescent so as to give play to the humanity. There must have been a decisive acceptance of the limitations imposed by human experience once for all.

> The Incarnate is God the Son, conditioned in and by manhood. His divine powers are always in His possession; but the conscious exercise of them is controlled by the law of restraint at the moment of the Incarnation (p. 204).
>
> By this law, the Incarnate has no possible means of self-knowledge or of the exercise of His divine powers that He cannot find in the manhood that He has assumed. . . . These means are not of fixed content, for, as the manhood grows and moves onwards to its glory, its power of mediating the divine must necessarily increase. But for ever the manhood is the measure of the self-consciousness and self-manifestation of the divine Son as Incarnate (p. 205).

The relation of the Son to the Father was, in the Incarnate life, a relation in and through the manhood. It was as one with us, from within our nature, that the Son had converse with the Father.

Weston is explicit where Gore had been vague. He helps us to conceive an immutable divine Sonship mediated within a genuinely human consciousness. The test lies in the application of the conception to the Gospel record: and no part of Weston's book is more valuable than the tracing of the main episodes in the life of Christ from the childhood to the Passion, shewing how we may think of the divine glory mediated through the human experiences and of the human nature being increasingly glorified the while. Where Weston's conception is vulnerable is that it perhaps fails to do justice to *all* the evidence in the Gospels, where there seem to be instances of a consciousness of divine power and sonship such as transcend the human limitations (cf. H. M. Relton, *A Study in Christology*, p. 218). But the strength of Weston's thesis is that it throws itself upon the Gospels for its verification, and bears that test to so considerable an extent. The book remains one of the greatest of all essays on the Incarnation.

Within the same decade non-Anglican theologians emerged with works on kenotic doctrine. If the best known among them was H. R. Mackintosh's *The Person of Jesus Christ* (1912), a book which Gore and Temple were to discuss as a foil to their own efforts, the greatest was P. T. Forsyth's *The Person and Place of Jesus Christ* (1909). Forsyth stands in sharp contrast with the Anglican writers whom we have been considering, and it was only in later years that Anglicans came to perceive his outstanding importance. (*a*) He approached the doctrine of the Incarnation from the evangelical standpoint of Redemption. He had written: 'There is in the Incarnation that which puts us at once at the moral heart of reality—the Son made sin rather than the Son made flesh. The Incarnation has no religious value but as the background of the atonement' (*Positive Preaching and Modern Mind*, p. 182). (*b*) The ancient formulations of substance, nature and person meant little to him. He lacked sympathy with the Fathers, feeling that these were prone to treat 'the Incarnation as an act largely metaphysical', which he contrasted with 'the moral act of atonement'. Yet it was just this ethical and evangelical emphasis which enabled him to treat the Incarnation with a rare profundity, and to draw out the kenotic doctrine no less movingly than Weston had done.

The utmost significance is to be attached to the pre-existence of the Son of God—Son in eternity no less than in time. There is the highest evangelical significance in the crucial (Forsyth would press the force of that adjective) act whereby the eternal Son became Man in time. 'His sacrifice began before He came into the world, and His Cross was that of a lamb slain before the world's foundation. There was a Calvary above which was the mother of it all. His obedience, however impressive, does not take divine magnitude if it first arose upon earth, nor has it the due compelling power upon ours. His obedience as man was but the detail of the supreme obedience which made him man' (*Person and Place of Jesus Christ*, p. 271). Yet the humanity of the Incarnate is no less significant. How then is the consciousness of Christ, not indeed intelligible, but credible? Forsyth insists on taking as the first step what he calls the 'moralizing of dogma'. Omnipotence and omniscience must be thought of not in *a priori* metaphysical terms, but as the Incarnation itself has disclosed them. *Omnipotence* is the limitless power of love: 'to appear and act as redeemer, to be born, suffer and die, was a mightier act of Godhead than lay in all the creation, preservation and blessing of the world' (p. 315). *Omniscience* is similarly the power of the infinite mind and will to share in the movement and discursiveness of the finite: 'The omniscience of God does not mean that it is incapable of limitation, but rather that, with more power than finitude has, it is also more capable of limitation. Only it is self-limitation: He limits Himself in the freedom of holiness for the purposes of His own end of infinite love' (p. 311). Thinking thus of the divine attributes, we may see how they are not renounced, but rather manifested, in the life and Passion of Christ, in a 'new man'. It was at once a movement of God manifesting power and knowledge within the life which was also a movement of Man towards self-realization. The union of God and Man is 'the mutual involution of two personal movements of the human soul and the divine' (p. 333). The kenosis and the plenosis went together. If Forsyth's description is rhetorical, it is neither more nor less explicit than the Johannine description of the Son of God who manifests His glory in the Passion and wins in the process of the earthly life the glory which is His already from all eternity.

It is in the course of this exposition that Forsyth treats characteristically the temptations of Christ. *Non potuit peccare*. 'He could be tempted because he loved: he could not sin, because he loved deeply' (p. 303). But, if He was thus sinless, could the trials be truly human? Yes, suggests Forsyth, 'What if his kenosis went so far that though the impossibility was there he did not know of it?'

In this study of Forsyth's book I have digressed from the specific story of Anglican theology. But Forsyth went perhaps further than any other theologian to relate kenotic doctrine to the fundamentals of theology. If he was prone to obscure metaphysics by rhetoric, and to surmount difficulties by paradox, it is perhaps in his hands that kenotic doctrine comes nearest to vindicating itself, and it is therefore perhaps by his version of it that it can claim most fairly to be judged.

III

It is evidence of the influence of kenotic doctrine, and not least of Charles Gore's effect upon Anglican thought, that Dr. Creed wrote in his Hulsean Lectures of 1938: 'Though kenotic doctrine is no longer so much in favour as it was, I should think it probable that a majority today of those among us who have a Christology which they are prepared to state and to defend, are still Kenoticists' (*The Divinity of Jesus Christ*, p. 75). Yet, before the date when those words were written, severe criticism of kenotic Christology had been made.

Some of the criticisms are applicable to the crude and extreme kenotic doctrines of the early phase; but do not seem to bear upon the doctrine as taught by Weston or Forsyth. Thus Dr. Rashdall wrote:

> According to Bishop Gore, the Word up to the moment of the Incarnation knew everything—all history, all modern science, all the undiscovered science that there is yet to know, the whole course of future history, so far at least as it is known to God the Father—but from the moment of the Incarnation He knew all this no more for some thirty-three years. Now it is surely a difficult doctrine to maintain that such a colossal loss of memory, such a complete break of consciousness in the Son was consistent with what we call personal identity. Certainly it is ridiculous to say that it is consistent with the Word being unchanged (*God and Man*, p. 95).

Two Consciousnesses

This criticism is not as devastating as it might seem, if close attention is given to what Forsyth had to say about omnipotence and omniscience working through the limitations of love.

But the most significant criticism came from William Temple in his *Christus Veritas*, published in 1924 when he was Bishop of Manchester. Temple was unwilling to follow the idea of kenosis.

> The difficulties [he says] are intolerable. What was happening to the rest of the universe during the period of our Lord's earthly life? To say that the Infant Jesus was from His cradle exercising providential government over it all is certainly monstrous; but to deny this, and yet to say that the Creative Word was so self-emptied as to have no being except in the Infant Jesus, is to assert that for a certain period the world was let loose from the control of the creative Word, and 'apart from Him' very nearly everything happened that happened at all during thirty odd years, both on this planet, and throughout the immensities of space (pp. 142–143).

Furthermore, Temple urged that the idea of kenosis made the period of the Incarnation a mere episode in the life of the Godhead—whereas it was truly an episode revealing and symbolic of God as He eternally is, shewing us what God is ever and always like in the glory of His self-giving love. As an alternative to kenosis, Temple suggested: 'All these difficulties are avoided if we suppose that God the Son did most truly live the life recorded in the Gospel, but added to this the other work of God. There are indications that this is the Johannine view' (p. 143).

Yet if Temple's alternative removes difficulties it seems to create new ones. It has not been hard to point those out. As Quick said, does not the *addition* of the human experiences to the life of the divine Word itself imply the addition of what are in effect *limitations* (*Doctrines of the Creed*, pp. 136–139). And as has been said both by Quick and by J. M. Creed (*Mysterium Christi*, p. 135), does not Temple's concept virtually involve a doctrine of two consciousnesses—unless the kenotic principle be applied?

I do not wish [says Creed] to be understood as myself arguing for a kenotic Christology, for I am moved by the considerations which Dr. Temple and others have urged against it. But I do not think that Dr. Temple shakes Professor Mackintosh's argument. If we take seriously both the human conditions of the life of Jesus and the theory of His personal identity and continuity with the eternal Word, then a kenotic Christology seems to be indispensable (op. cit., p. 136).

With Creed's testimony, and Quick's exposition, the doctrine of kenosis in its restrained and imprecise Anglican form, may be said to have held its own through fifty years.

IV

Today there is no doubt that kenotic doctrine has been more damaged by criticism of its metaphysical implications. Furthermore, the shift of theological interest has led to the kenotic question in any form receiving very much less attention. With less concern about the biographical aspect of the Gospels, and less willingness to give their minds to questions about the consciousness of Christ, theologians have been the more willing to rest in the affirmation of His deity and humanity, and to leave mystery at the core of the Gospel.[1]

To the Anglican theologians of the earlier period, however, the kenotic question inevitably loomed large. Given their adherence to the orthodoxy of the Person of the Word made flesh, and their concern for the human portrait in the Gospels, and given also the will to think in terms of consciousness characteristic of the time, the kenotic doctrine was to them almost a religious and theological necessity. What were the alternatives? To affirm the Deity of Christ in such wise as to make the humanity unreal, or to be content with an exclusively symbolic view of the Incarnation. According to such a view Jesus is the image of the invisible God, and in the man Jesus we find God

---

[1] Criticism of kenotic doctrine is to be found in D. M. Baillie, *God was in Christ*, pp. 94–98, E. L. Mascall, *Christ, the Christian and the Church*, pp. 23–33, and in a very valuable excursus by E. R. Fairweather in F. W. Beare, *A Commentary on the Epistle to the Philippians*.

Divine Humility

and worship Him. But to rest exclusively in this symbolic doctrine is to miss important factors in the apostolic teaching, not least the paradox of the divine act of humility whereby the eternal Word was made flesh. It is to this aspect of the Incarnation that Anglican theology has adhered with special tenacity, and it was its adherence to it which caused the kenotic question to be prominent in its own time. Hooker, Andrewes, Liddon, Church, Gore and Temple, despite the differences between them, are at one in a passionate emphasis upon the divine humility in the act which evokes the depth of man's adoration of *Verbum Caro Factum*. None had dwelt upon the divine humility more movingly than had Pusey, who in his sermon, 'The Incarnation, a Lesson of Humility', echoed the words of S. Augustine, 'tantum te pressit humana superbia, ut te non posset nisi humilitas sublevare divina', 'so deeply had human pride sunk us, that nothing but Divine Humility could raise us'.[1]

[1] Augustine, Sermon 188, quoted Pusey, *Sermons from Advent to Whitsuntide*.

CHAPTER FOUR

THE DOCTRINE OF THE CROSS

I

IT has become a commonplace to say that in the Anglican theology characteristic of our period the Atonement was very far from the centre. So much was this so that we are conscious when we approach the time of the Second World War that a return to a theology of Redemption is on the way. Yet, the Cross always had its place in the religion of the great teachers of our period, and in retrospect it is apparent that some significant essays in the interpretation of the Cross were made, preparing the way for subsequent doctrinal synthesis. Two facts had much influence in this process. One was the hold of Anglican devotion upon the sacrificial aspect of the Eucharist. The other was the deepened reflection about suffering and evil which came with the agonies of the First World War.

As so often, Henry Scott Holland was prophetic of what was to follow. Far back in the eighteen-eighties his sermons in S. Paul's had shewn some of those lightning-flashes so characteristic of him. In *Logic and Life* (1883), a remarkable sermon on 'Christ the Justification of a Suffering World', shews how a law of sacrifice pervades the story of nature and man, with Calvary and the New Man in Christ as the climax. Destruction and growth, death and life, waste and recovery run through the story of the world, of ancient life, of the emergence of Man. But is Man, as he is, the goal—Man with his tale of advance and decay? 'Man cannot find in himself the worth of all this age-long sacrifice.' Then come the Jews—witnessing through their own story of death and life that *holiness, righteousness*, are worth all that has gone before. But how are holiness, righteousness realized on earth? In 'the holy image of God's perfect

Theological Wisdom

righteousness, taking upon Himself the whole agony of man . . . and turning death itself into the instrument of the higher inheritance'. The discourse ends with an invocation of Jesus: 'Fill us with thy sorrow, if so only thou canst fill us with thyself.' I must needs think that this sermon is among the greatest of all time. In prose rhetorical and yet perlucid it anticipates the theological wisdom which the toil of several decades was to work out.

There follows a series of four sermons on 'Sacrifice': 'the sacrifice of Innocence', 'the sacrifice of the Fallen', 'the sacrifice of the Man', 'the sacrifice of the Redeemed'. (1) Holland begins with the term 'sacrifice' used in the ideal sense (as it had been used by S. Augustine and by F. D. Maurice, though he quotes neither) of Man's happy relation of dependence, homage, self-donation, towards his Creator: 'Even if no dividing sin had ever severed man and God, still religion would consist in the joy of self-dedication, the joy of homage, the joy of an offering, the joy of a sacrifice. There would still be the altar and still the priest; an altar of joy, and gladness, and thanksgiving and praise. . . .'[1] (2) But sin and death have supervened, the scene has darkened; and in the world as we know it there is not the ideal sacrifice but the sacrifice of the Fallen. 'Sacrifice can only be now a recovery of allegiance . . . from the sad and ruinous sense of finding himself outside God . . . the sense of severance, the sense of death.' What, then, can Man offer? Only 'the offering of that very sense of death, which drags into ruin all this life'. (3) And who can offer that truly? We come to the 'sin-bearing' sacrifice of Christ, for Christ 're-dedicates for man that very torment of death which he had suffered in penalty of sin'. (4) Finally, there can follow the sacrifice of the Redeemed, for 'Christ's sacrifice is no far-away fact to be shown and gazed upon. It draws us also into itself'.

Let these sentences be added from another of Holland's volumes, *Creed and Character* (1887). 'He sends His Son, in whom

---

[1] Cf. Augustine, *De Civitate Dei*, X, Ch. vi: 'Sacrifice is every deed that is done to the end that we may cleave to God in fellowship in relation to that good end by which we might become blessed.'

His forgiveness can find a road into the repellent earth, into this repugnant humanity. . . . God's forgiveness issues out of heaven in the shape of a Man, wearing human flesh. Jesus Christ is the Forgiveness of the Father. He arrives bringing with Him the pardon of the Father, and the pardon is effectual. For there is now in Man one spot on which the eyes of God's purity can rest. . . . Christ, the Forgiveness, *becomes the one forgiven Man*.' This is another of Holland's lightning-flashes: it anticipates in a phrase the theme of R. C. Moberly's great book.

Among the writings of the *Lux Mundi* group there was one monograph on the Atonement, R. C. Moberly's *Atonement and Personality* (1901). It stands apart with a certain loneliness alike in achievement and in failure. To read it is still a searching experience. It belongs to the literature of spirituality no less than to the literature of dogmatics.

Moberly wrote somewhat in reaction from R. W. Dale, the Congregationalist divine whose modified treatment of the penal theory in his *The Atonement* (1875) held the field as the ablest modern exposition of an evangelical doctrine. Moberly thought that Dale had left the Atonement too much as a transaction outside us without shewing its impact upon us through the work of the Holy Spirit. It is here that Moberly's strength lay: if he dwelt upon the manward side of the Atonement, and did so even in psychological terms, it was because he could not separate in thought the questions 'What was the Atonement in relation to God and the world?' and 'What actually happens in the souls of men?'

The concepts 'punishment', 'penitence', 'forgiveness' are to be defined in terms of their complete manifestation and result. *Punishment* is in its first incidence retributive, but its proper goal is that 'the pain endured is taken up into the change of self which we call penitence'. *Penitence* is sorrow for sin, but sinful habit blunts its edge and dims its power—leaving us with the paradox that 'the consummation of penitence would be possible only to the absolutely sinless'. *Forgiveness* too is 'inchoate': 'it is the recognition indeed of something in the present—but a

The Perfect Penitent

something whose real significance lies in the undeveloped possibilities of the future. It is not consummated perfectly till the forgiven man is righteous.' Somewhat unconvincing in the logic of his definitions, and still more unconvincing in relation to the Biblical usage of the words (which indeed he never really examines), Moberly goes on to use a very convincing, true-to-life analogy of a parent and a child. The parent must disown the child's wrongdoing, with the love that can never wholly identify the child with the wrongdoing. The love cannot be translated into forgiveness so long as the child is self-identified with its passion. So soon as there is the first dim touch or gleam of child-like regret and sorrow, the action of forgiveness can begin in turn to deepen the sorrow through which the will towards good returns. And it is possible for the parent to feel the sorrow as a godly sorrow more fully than the child at first can do.

I have never felt sure how far either the definitions or the analogy really serve Moberly's central thesis: Christ the Perfect Penitent. In Christ alone there was, as Man and for Mankind, that perfect act of sorrow for sin, which sinful men can themselves never feel or achieve as they should, the perfect sacrifice for sin. 'Only He, who knew in Himself the measure of the holiness of God, could realize also, in the human nature He had made His own, the full depth of the alienation of sin from God, the real character of the penal averting of God's face.'[1] But Christ's perfect penitence is not the end. The perfect sorrow for sin which we can never feel, and the alienation of the will from sin which we can never achieve, these gifts are now brought to us by the Risen Christ and given to us by the Holy Spirit. 'The very spirit of the Crucified becomes our spirit: ourselves translated into the spirit of the Crucified. The spirit of the Crucified

---

[1] Moberly's conception was in succession to that of McLeod Campbell in *The Nature of the Atonement* (1856), 'that oneness of mind with the Father, which towards man took the form of condemnation of sin, would in the Son's dealing with the Father in the relation to our sins, take the form of a perfect confession of our sins. This confession, as to its own nature, must have been a perfect Amen in humanity to the judgment of God on the sin of man' (p. 135).

may be, and please God shall be, the very constituting reality of ourselves.' 'The spirit of human penitence could not be ours, till penitence had been realized in humanity. The spirit of human righteousness could not be ours, till humanity, in the consummation of penitence, had become perfectly one with the righteousness of God.' There follow chapters on the Spirit, on freedom and grace, on Church and sacraments; chapters dependent upon the main theme and yet of high value even without it. The goal is man's self-realization, 'I, yet not I. Not I, and therefore the full, real, consummated, "I" at last.'

Moberly's thesis met formidable criticism. It was questioned whether his view of penitence as a state wherein the soul grows by grace is not more the child of Catholic piety than of New Testament teaching. Is not the inadequacy of repentance of its essence, as a man throws himself before the Cross of Christ knowing that the conflict of impulses within him is unresolved, and pleading for mercy, 'just as he is'? Again, it was questioned whether the view of forgiveness as an ideal state to be realized is not far from the Biblical proclamation of forgiveness as itself the beginning of Christian life: 'My little children, I write unto you, because your sins are forgiven you for his name's sake.' If those criticisms could be made by contemporary theologians, still more today, when the more comprehensive conspectus of the doctrine of redemption has returned, does Moberly's book seem preoccupied with a psychological point of reference in contrast with the Biblical theme of cosmic deliverance through Christ's death and resurrection. His theme stands rather lonely.

Yet a wealth of pastoral experience will echo Moberly's theme with gratitude. How often does a man say 'I want to be sorry for my sin—but I find I cannot be: I want to confess my sin, but I know not how'! The fragmentary movements of penitence in the soul become stifled as soon as they are born, whether by the lethargy which cannot face sorrow at all or the self-pity which misdirects it. How often then has the wise pastor or evangelist shewn that we cannot sorrow for our sins as we should: there is only Christ's perfect sorrow for them, and our

Original Sin

sorrow is learnt from Him and received by us as a tiny fragment of His. Repentance and forgiveness are by grace alone: and there is not only the grace of Christ Who pardons us, there is no less the grace of Christ Who is at our side in our contrition and confession—making it with us, and for us, *Christus totus in nostris*.

Dated, if we care to say so, by its psychological reference and by its distance from the main exposition of the Biblical terms, Moberly's book had a big influence in the practical presentation of the atonement in parochial teaching, in evangelism, in the cure of souls. It is indeed within the life of the soul that the 'Biblical and eschatological drama' (to use a description of what Moberly is accused of neglecting) can and does happen. In the words of Scott Holland which I have already quoted, 'Fill us with thy sorrow, if so only thou canst fill us with thyself'.

II

Charles Gore, unlike R. C. Moberly, wrote no treatise on the Atonement; and in the shape of his writings the Incarnation was central. Yet the whole of his theology took its tone from the theme of sin and redemption. 'Everything in the New Testament', he could write, 'appears to depend on this initial sacrifice of atonement, reconciliation and propitiation.' [1]

It was his sense of the gravity of sin which was for Gore the dividing line between his understanding of the Incarnation and that of much contemporary liberalism. He thought of this gravity both as that of the guilt of the individual for his own sins of wilfulness, and that of the collective taint in the race known as 'original sin'. The story of Adam and Eve was a myth, symbolizing both aspects of the matter. 'Sin is in the race before it is in the individual will, and every individual is born into an inheritance of sin.' [2] Not responsible for the taint of sin, the individual is guilty of his own measure of yielding to it. With an equal emphasis upon the individual and collective aspects of

[1] *The Reconstruction of Belief*, p. 589.
[2] *The New Theology and the Old Religion*, p. 74.

sin, Gore is equally emphatic about redemption as the personal forgiveness of the individual and as his incorporation within the new redeemed race in Christ the New Man.

Redemption flows from the initiative of God's love: there is no propitiation requisite to elicit that love. But the initiative of God's love issues in Christ's sacrifice for sin, because the *corporate* nature of redemption requires a covenant sacrifice as its basis, because the *holiness* of God requires a condemnation of sin in the very act by which it is forgiven, and because the *obedience* of man can be restored only by the perfect obedience of Christ amid the conditions of a sinful and suffering world. All these elements are included alike in the necessity of Christ's sacrifice, and in its interpretation. Noteworthy is Gore's exposition of propitiation in his Westminster Abbey Lectures on the Epistle to the Romans: 'The awful burden laid upon Jesus on account of human sin, the awful sacrifice of His life which He readily offered, restores the sterner element to our thoughts about God, just at that crisis or opportunity in the divine dealings, when by God's declaration of free forgiveness we are made to feel His love. God does forgive us, but it costs Him much' (p. 184). But not less noteworthy is Gore's insistence that, while there is a moral necessity in Christ's death, it is proper to speak of *vicarious sacrifice* but unwarranted to speak of *vicarious punishment*. Thus Gore could find no place either for penal substitution or for the idea of Christ as the perfect penitent: neither conception seemed to him to accord with Scripture or with reason. His mind was wont to shrink from paradox.

It is striking indeed that a school of theology so avowedly incarnational could produce expositions of atonement as deep, original and comprehensive as those of Holland, Moberly and Gore. To all of them the Eucharist was a constant interpreter of doctrine, and the Eucharist enabled them to see the doctrine in terms cosmic and liturgical, no less than evangelical. Mankind's deliverance into salvation means the recovery of the creaturely adoration of a Creator. The song of the redeemed is the recapture of the Song of creation.

The heavenly priesthood of Christ had been a theme for

A Priestly Rôle

many Anglican writers, going back to Jeremy Taylor. Moberly drew out this theme in the last chapter of his *Ministerial Priesthood* (1897). Like Westcott, he understood 'the blood' to mean not the death in itself, but the life that has passed through death. Unlike Westcott, he was able to speak of the life being perpetually 'offered'—construing 'offering' to mean the self-giving of love which is eternally characteristic of One who is Priest and Son, and is now marked by the death once died and never repeatable.

> Christ's offering in Heaven is a perpetual ever-present offering of life, whereof 'to have died' is an ever-present and perpetual attribute. If 'Calvary' were the sufficient statement of the nature of the sacrifice of Christ, then the sacrifice would be simply done and past, which is in truth both now and ever present. He is a Priest for ever, not as it were by a perpetual series of acts of memory, not by multiplied and ever remoter acts of commemoration of a death that is past, but by the eternal presentation of a life which is eternally the 'life that died' (p. 246).

A line of Anglican writers made this theme their own, not least H. B. Swete in very cautious and careful language in *The Ascended Christ*. And aided by the hymns of William Bright and Charles Wesley, worshippers have learned that the Eucharist on earth is one with the heavenly altar. United thus to the great High Priest the Church on earth has a priestly rôle: 'the Church is priestly', in Moberly's words, 'because from her proceeds the aroma of perpetual offering towards God. The Church is priestly because her arms are spread out perpetually to succour and intercede for those who need the sacrifice of love.'

But how does the Eucharist unite the Church with Christ's one sacrifice? The Eucharist itself not being here our theme, what is said must needs be brief. The first of modern Anglicans to write of this fully was Gore, in *The Body of Christ* (1901). His thought is in line with Holland's: 'the setting free of humanity to offer the sacrifices proper to man, not because he is a trembling sinner, but because he is a forgiven and accepted son and knows what he owes to God for his creation and his redemption'. These sacrifices are co-extensive with the entire life of the

Church, but the Eucharist is their focus—for the Church dare not offer them except in union with Christ's perpetual presentation of the sacrifice which He made on Calvary. What then is the connection? Gore appeals to two lines of thought in the Christian tradition. (1) There is the doctrine that the offerings of bread and wine are accepted at the heavenly altar and united to Christ's heavenly offering, and given back as Christ's body and blood to be the food of the people. (2) There is the doctrine that, in virtue of the consecration, the sacrifice of Christ is present in our midst, and it is *this* which we present before the Father (having with us Christ, who was once crucified and ever lives, offering the life that died). The two doctrines may, in Gore's view, be complementary: but neither is complete without the corollary that sacrifice is perfected in Communion. Here Gore draws upon the teaching of S. Augustine that 'if you have received well, you are what you have received.... He willed that we ourselves should be His sacrifice' (Augustine, *Sermons*, 227); 'this is the Christian sacrifice, the many become one body in Christ' (*De Civitate Dei*, X, 20).

Such is Gore's outline of the doctrine of Eucharistic sacrifice, yet it left gaps to be filled by writers in later decades. There were those who, like F. C. N. Hicks, former Bishop of Lincoln, put the weight emphatically upon the heavenly offering: in his book the *Fulness of Sacrifice* (1930) the strength is a comprehensive sweep of treatment worthy of Scott Holland, the weakness is an over-pressing of 'the blood is the life'. Others have dwelt upon the sacrifice being pre-eminently the sacrifice of the Passion. No treatment on these lines is more significant than that by Sir Will Spens in *Essays Catholic and Critical* (1926). It resembles without, however, any dependence the teaching of the French theologian de la Taille. Spens' theme is that every Eucharist, like the Last Supper, invests our Lord's death with sacrificial significance, so that the one unrepeatable fact of Calvary is kept at the heart of our approach to God. Both these presentations of sacrifice incurred hostility from those who think that they impugn the all-sufficiency of the one sacrifice of the Cross. In fact, for such writers, as for Holland, Moberly and

Anglicans and the Atonement

Gore, the Eucharistic sacrifice is a supreme assertion of the all-sufficiency of the Cross, utterly congruous with Justification by Faith Alone.

> Look, Father, look on His anointed face,
> And only look on us as found in Him.

III

In Anglican teaching on the Atonement in the 'nineties and the first two decades of the present century, there were two chief types. There were evangelicals who taught a strict doctrine of penal substitution, dwelling upon what Christ endured in our stead in order that we might be saved. Bishop Handley Moule of Durham could write moving expositions, at once devout and scholarly, of the meaning of Faith in Christ who bore our penalty on the Cross;[1] and he supplemented them by his admirable book on the Holy Spirit, *Veni Creator*. But these works were slight, and the great theological treatment of this aspect of Atonement came from Scotland and the Free Churches. Dale's book long continued to have influence, and so did the books of P. T. Forsyth and James Denney. On the other hand, there were those who, standing within the Catholic Movement, taught the Atonement in terms of sacrifice in its several stages and found in Eucharistic worship a constant influence upon the preaching of the Cross. Christ offered the perfect sacrifice which mankind was incapable of offering, so that now—cleansed by His blood and incorporated into Him—we may offer ourselves in Him.

In the first two decades of the century both these traditional types of doctrine found themselves in conflict with a doctrine in vogue within the liberalism of the time: an exclusively exemplarist, manward or Abelardian view of Atonement. It was of course presentations of traditional doctrine which lacked a right comprehensiveness, with a narrow concentration upon a godward transaction, that caused exemplarist doctrine to make

[1] Cf. H. C. G. Moule, *The Epistle to the Romans* (The Expositors' Bible); *Faith*; *Outlines of Christian Doctrine*.

The Doctrine of the Cross

its appeal to devout and critical minds. The greatest work of the modern Abelardian type was *The Idea of Atonement in Christian Theology* by Hastings Rashdall, the Bampton Lectures for 1915. It is a learned history of the doctrine through nineteen centuries, and it has taken long for more learned monographs on particular parts of the field to make Rashdall's book no longer indispensable. But, considered purely as an historical work, it has a revealing weakness. In discussing theories which are unacceptable, whether because they were intellectually 'dated' or because they failed to do justice to Christian truth, Rashdall seldom probes to the religious need or the theological instinct which lay beneath the particular theory. Was it mere perversity which caused a Gregory of Nyssa, an Anselm or a Luther to say what they did? Furthermore, in the field of exegesis there is in the book an arbitrariness congruous with the criticism which saw Christian origins in rigidly separate strata: *nothing* in the way of ransom-doctrine, or covenant-blood doctrine or the use of Isaiah 53, is to be ascribed to our Lord; *all* is a construction originating in the early Church.

Rashdall's doctrine was thus summarized:

> The Church's early Creed 'There is none other name given among men by which we may be saved' will be translated so as to be something of this kind: 'There is none other ideal given among men by which we may be saved except the moral ideal which Christ taught by His words, and illustrated by His life and death of love; and there is none other help so great in the attainment of that ideal as the belief in God as He had been supremely revealed in Him who so taught and lived and died.' So understood, the self-sacrificing life which was consummated by the death upon the Cross has, indeed, power to take away the sins of the whole world.'

It is interesting that the most penetrating comment on Rashdall's doctrine was made by one of the most genuinely liberal of theologians of the time, John Oman. After pointing out that though he rejected all mediaeval doctrines of merit, Rashdall leaves us in the end with a pure doctrine of merit whereby we find our own way to salvation by our good lives done in the imitation of Christ's example, Oman says:

The Penal Theory

Neither the honest blundering of Dr. Dale, nor the passionate scholarship of Dr. Denney, nor the super-subtlety of Dr. Forsyth, nor the refined elusiveness of Dr. Moberly, can any more put reality into the penal theory. Nevertheless, one has a feeling that all these writers are reaching out after some spiritual need with which Dr. Rashdall is untroubled, not because he has solved the problem, but because he has ignored it. So far as he goes he is wholly right, and until his criticism is accepted a sound theology convincing by its own veracity is impossible. But when one compares him with St. Paul, or even with Luther, one realizes how little he cares to live in the half lights, and how all really creative souls have to live there all the time (*Journal of Theological Studies*, April 1921).

'To put life into the penal theory.' There were Anglican scholars, quite distinct from the old evangelical school, who were prepared to do this, avoiding the crudities of substitutionism, and remembering that what Christ did 'for us' is inseparable from what Christ does 'in us'. Such an one was J. K. Mozley, Canon of S. Paul's, an Anglican disciple of Forsyth; and his *The Doctrine of the Atonement* (1917) and *The Heart of the Gospel* (1925) shew a catholicity which vibrates with evangelical passion. On the other hand, K. E. Kirk, in his essay on 'Atonement' in *Essays Catholic and Critical*, and in a long discussion of Pauline theology in a commentary on *Romans* (1937), argued that only the slenderest basis, if any, can be found for substitutionism in S. Paul and that the New Testament doctrine may be best summed up in the admittedly non-Biblical word 'reparation'. It is important to notice where these writers, belonging as they did to the Catholic Anglican school, stand in relation to Reformation issues. This can be seen in their attitude to Justification. While being at pains to disclaim the narrow solifidianism which it was customary to ascribe to Luther, and to dwell upon the completion of justification in sanctification, these writers would none the less interpret the *term* 'justification' in the Reformation rather than in the Tridentine sense, as God's acceptance of sinful men solely on the basis of Christ's merits through their faith. Such had been the lines of Charles Gore's exposition of Romans 3: 21–26, in his Westminster Abbey

Lectures, and such, too, was to be William Temple's line when he wrote in *Christus Veritas* (p. 262): 'In so far as the term "propitiation" represents something objectively accomplished in and by God Himself . . . to that extent it is the term which, of all that are open to us, carries us farthest into the meaning of the Atonement.'

The greatest defence of a doctrine is its creative exposition, and in due time scholarship was able to draw together different elements in the understanding of the Atonement and present in the doctrine with a fresh comprehensiveness. This was done with success by O. C. Quick in his systematic work, *The Doctrines of the Creed* (1937), and in his monograph, *The Gospel of the New World* (1944). Quick, who held the Chair of Divinity at Durham before becoming Regius Professor of Divinity at Oxford in 1939, was a philosophical theologian not unlike William Temple in method. But whereas Temple proceeded from a particular philosophical discipline to Christian theology, Quick was primarily a theologian who proceeded from the Biblical revelation (though he would in no sense claim to be a Biblical scholar) to its consequences for metaphysics. He resembled Temple in his devotion to the task of analysis and synthesis: and he pursued that task in his *Catholic and Protestant Elements in Christianity* (1922) and his *The Christian Sacraments* (1927). But nowhere, I think, did he follow this method more successfully than in that part of his work in systematic theology which concerns atonement and eschatology, and in the drawing together of these two themes he was expressing in doctrinal exposition the newer trends in Biblical studies.

There had been a revival, in the work of Gustav Aulén of Lund, of the 'classic' doctrine of Atonement as the victory of God in Christ over cosmic powers of evil—a doctrine held both by many ancient Fathers and by Luther. There had been a new emphasis in New Testament studies upon the 'new age' inaugurated by Christ's messianic mission. There had been no less a new interest in the idea of covenant sacrifice at the Last Supper as the key to that mission. Quick shewed how these doctrines cohere, if the concept of sacrifice is kept at the centre.

Divine Justice

Sacrificial images from the Old Testament, in being fulfilled in Christ, are blended and their meaning is transformed. Thus, Christ is *both* the pure victim offered as a cleansing sacrifice *and* the unholy scapegoat bearing sin upon Himself: it is a paradoxical combination—yet He is never more the one than when He is the other, since the love whereby He offers a pure obedience to the Father is the self-same love whereby He bears man's sin and shame. Again, Christ is both the victorious king and the sacrificial victim: and both are of one, since the sacrifice is itself the victorious power. Again, His Cross demonstrates the divine justice—because it issues in the actual deliverance of mankind into the world-to-come. Again, Christ bears our penalty, but does so in such wise that the death that is penal is also sacrificial—issuing in the acceptance of the 'blood' in the Resurrection. The Resurrection is the climax of sacrifice, in that the sacrificial blood is thereby accepted and made available in its cleansing power: but this is only another way of saying that the Resurrection is the beginning of a new creation.

By this means, Quick is able to shew that each of the doctrines which had come in the course of history to be isolated and systematized apart from the others ('classic', 'satisfaction', 'penal', 'exemplarist') has its place within a larger whole.[1] What is true in all of them can be held together so long as we keep at the centre the concept of sacrifice, to be seen both in the comprehensiveness of its Old Testament presentation, and in the light of its refashioning by the death and resurrection of Christ. Such is atonement, evangelical, cosmic, liturgical, as indeed Scott Holland had prophetically hinted, and as the Eucharist is always at hand to interpret it.

[1] Cf. *Gospel of the New World*, p. 103. 'Abelardian theories are true so far as they go. The Cross and resurrection are indeed the unique demonstration of God's eternal love for man. But they are that demonstration, just because they are infinitely more than a mere demonstration. They bring into being the manhood of the world to come, the first fruits of the new creation, the sacrificed and living manhood of Christ, who through that manhood has become the head of His Church.'

The Doctrine of the Cross

IV

Does God suffer? Traditional theology, patristic, scholastic and reformed alike, had said that God is impassible. The question is too vast for us to discuss again here and now. But as we are sketching the history of Anglican teaching about the Cross we have to notice the tendency, especially in the nineteen-twenties, to believe that the traditional doctrine of impassibility must be modified and that God suffers. In popular teaching this view had come to the fore in Studdert-Kennedy's preaching and verses at the time of the 1914-1918 war. His book *The Hardest Part*, written for readers sensitive to the agony of the world, spoke of God as the greatest sufferer of all. Philosophically, patripassianism was upheld by C. F. D'Arcy, Archbishop of Dublin, in *God and the Struggle for Existence*, a volume to which B. H. Streeter also contributed. But theologically the most prominent teaching on these lines was in William Temple's *Christus Veritas*. It was teaching evoked no doubt by sensitivity to the distresses of the time, and congruous with the Hegelian strain in Temple's thought; but its root is in the plain theological insistence that Christ is the key to God as He eternally is, the Cross is 'the unveiling of a mystery of the Divine Life itself— the revelation of the cost whereby God wins victory over the evil which He had permitted' (p. 262). 'All that we can suffer of physical or mental anguish is within the divine experience; He has known it all Himself.' There is a true sense in which God is 'without Passions', for He is never 'Passive' in the sense of having things happen to Him except with His consent; but the traditional term really meant 'incapable of suffering', and this Temple says is 'almost wholly false'. 'Almost'! In that word there is on Temple's part a slight drawing back: and he seems to explain the 'almost' by the sentence 'It is truer to say that there is suffering in God than that God suffers.' And why? 'the suffering is an element in the joy of the triumphant sacrifice'.

It is significant that while the argument, and in large measure the religious instinct in *Christus Veritas* led Temple towards the

'Suffering and God'

assertion of divine suffering, there is yet this holding back. God suffers, not as one who is thwarted: but as one who wills to suffer in His purpose as supreme Creator and victorious Redeemer; and if we say that He suffers we may never pity Him, for we are worshippers of Him in a perfection beyond all our imagining. Equally characteristic of Anglican divinity have been both the move towards patripassianism and the drawing back: indeed, the double movement has sometimes been seen within the working of the mind of a single theologian. The first betokens the Christocentric strain in our theology: the drawing back betokens the sense of mystery and the sense of the adoration of the Creator in His perfection springing from our tradition of worship. It may be possible to exaggerate, and yet it is wrong to belittle the extent of Baron von Hügel's influence in this regard: but the influence was there, and not least in the essay on 'Suffering and God' which became well known in Anglican circles through its inclusion in the second published series of *Essays and Addresses* (1926), the year after *Christus Veritas*. This essay goes deep into the implications of man's creatureliness and God's perfection. No Anglican could easily write, as von Hügel wrote, of the divine 'isness', or say that the 'thirst of religion is, at bottom, a metaphysical thirst'. Yet von Hügel influenced Anglicans so greatly because his teaching was congruous with that unity of theology and worship always latent in our tradition. The gratitude of the redeemed to their Redeemer for what He has done is interpenetrated by the creature's adoration of the Creator in the perfection of His Being.

CHAPTER FIVE

MODERNISM

I

THE *Lux Mundi* school had made it possible for many to take rest in the belief that critical study and orthodox faith could go hand in hand. The marriage appeared for a while to escape undue strains, partly because it had been the criticism of the Old Testament which was mainly the issue, and partly because the criticism of the New Testament which was conspicuous in this country up to the turn of the century was mainly of a conservative and reassuring kind. But while some of the older Broad Church critical spirit had been absorbed into the *Lux Mundi* school, and had therein found contentment, there remained the Broad Churchmen proper, radical and unappeased, the parents of what the new century was to know as Modernism.

Modernism in the Church of England inherited the older Broad Church spirit: the desire to separate inward religion from dogma, to study the Bible like any other book, to free the consciences of churchmen from rigid interpretations of subscription or from subscription itself, to keep the national Church as comprehensive as was the variety of religious outlook among the English people. How various the Broad Churchmen could be is seen in the contrast of Jowett, devoted to philosophic speculation, utterly detached from interest in doctrines and religious institutions, and, when asked what would be his attitude to subscription, saying only, 'Give me a pen'; and Stanley, the man of historical imagination, fascinated by the study of religious confessions and institutions, and eager to reform them. Modernism inherited something of both those attitudes, but fed itself from newer trends of the twentieth century, and not least

Liberal Protestantism

from a powerful school of continental thought. This, however, was what was known not as Modernism, but Liberal Protestantism.

II

Near the beginning of the century the normal isolation of English theology from the Continent was contradicted by some names which became household words for the English student: Harnack, Schweitzer, Loisy. It is the first of these names which most concerns English Modernism. It had been the teaching of Albrecht Ritschl of Bonn and Göttingen (1822-1889) that we can speak about the significance of Jesus only in terms of the impact of His historical life upon the conscience, an impact which elicits from us a 'value-judgment' that for us He has 'the value of God'. Metaphysical propositions or dogmatic formulations concerning Christ are meaningless. To this school belonged Adolf Harnack (1851-1930), who became, as a Professor in Berlin, one of the most influential German divines of the time. In a famous course of lectures given in Berlin in 1901 with the title *Das Wesen des Christentums*[1] he gave what came to be known as a classic exposition of 'Liberal Protestantism' in the technical sense which the term was acquiring. The essence of Christianity lay in the teaching of Jesus in Galilee about the Kingdom of God, which was received and entered by those who accepted the Fatherhood of God with its corollary, the brotherhood of man. That was the core of the Gospel. The doctrines of Christology and of atonement taught by the apostles were false accretions, and the beginnings of a process whereby the simple Gospel of Jesus was elaborated into an Hellenistic theology. We must go behind this process and discover the true Jesus, and thus complete the work of the Reformation by removing the remains of the husk so that the kernel will be plain to see. The Liberal Protestant view had behind it the work of a number of critical scholars who concluded that the elements in the Gospel tradition which contained high Christology, or miracle, or

[1] The English translation bore the title *What is Christianity?*

atonement doctrine or supernaturalism represented not what Jesus really did or taught but later interpretations of Him read back into the story from the standpoint of the developing theology of the Church. When once the axiom of this progressive development was established, it seemed scientific to let this axiom govern the treatment of critical questions.

In England there came to be reproduced, amid the different conditions of English scholarship and piety, something akin to Harnack, both in critical method and in religious attitude. The phrase 'the Jesus of history' came to be the symbol of a way of regarding the Gospels. It meant the attempt to reconstruct the picture of Jesus as He was, on the assumptions that the apostolic theology was largely a distortion of His own original Gospel, and that the supernaturalism in the records is largely unhistorical. Many presentations of the life of Jesus were written on these lines, the most influential being T. R. Glover's *The Jesus of History* (1917).

Within the ambit of Liberal Protestantism in England, however, there was also a type of Christology both more positive in its content and theological in its presentation. I would like to take a leap forward in time and ask you to have a glimpse at the presentation of Christ by B. H. Streeter in his attractive book *Reality* (1926). Jesus by the perfection of His humanity reflects and embodies creative love, which is the explanation of the world order and the essence of God's nature. Thus He is God, evoking from us the adoration due only to Deity. Such is a view of the Incarnation which may be called strictly and exclusively 'symbolical'. It is in line with much which we find within the New Testament. It is congruous with the adoration of Jesus as divine. But if a Christology goes no further, it appears vulnerable as soon as certain questions are asked. (1) What is unique and unrepeatable about Jesus? Is it not necessary to emphasize the unique thing which He *did* as redeemer as well as His rôle as a symbol, if the full significance of His deity is to be stated? (2) Is there not a wedge, or at least a gap, between Jesus and the revelation in Israel which preceded Him and the subsequent apostolic interpretation of Him? Yet along Streeter's route

Catholic Modernism

many found their way to the divine Christ, and who should repel them?

We must, however, retrace our steps to the first years of the century, and to the Continent. While Harnack was lecturing in Berlin on 'What is Christianity?' Schweitzer was writing in Strassburg his very different interpretation of Jesus, as the apocalyptic teacher who proclaimed the imminence of the end, and died of a broken heart with the expectation unfulfilled. Schweitzer's fascinating thesis cannot now detain us,[1] except inasmuch as it was used by Alfred Loisy, whose name introduces another movement, Catholic Modernism, a movement of much consequence for our present theme. Loisy, a Roman Catholic scholar at the Institut Catholique in Paris, had been engaging in critical studies of the Bible in a way which drew the hostility of Roman Catholic authority. The movement which sprang from him involved also George Tyrrell, an Irish Jesuit who had been an Anglican, and—though with deep misgivings—Baron von Hügel. The crushing of this movement by Papal authority did not rob it of its significance for theology or of its influence upon Anglican thought.

Loisy's problem was how to reconcile radical criticism of the Gospels and loyalty to Catholic faith. He gave his answer in the form of a reply to Harnack in his book, *L'Évangile et l'Église* (1902). By the use of a critical evaluation of the Gospel record akin to Schweitzer's, he disallowed Harnack's picture of the message of Jesus. The Kingdom of God as taught by Jesus was eschatological: it was not an inward righteousness, but an event of the Messiah coming to reign on earth, and repentance and righteousness are demanded of those who would enter that Kingdom. But what was that Kingdom to be? Here, says Loisy, the Gospels shew only the preliminary part of the picture, for the Kingdom was to be embodied in the Catholic Church which developed from the Gospel and fulfilled and cleansed the Greek mystery-religions just as it fulfilled and cleansed the Jewish tradition. The fulness of truth is seen not in origins, but in

[1] See Appendix A for a note on Schweitzer's influence upon Anglican thought.

development; and the eschatological message of Jesus came to be translated into other forms more fit for it as the universal religion and Church. It was a startling thesis. Historical criticism was so used as to establish as cardinal the apocalyptic Gospel which Harnack had rejected, and then to explain, as Harnack had failed to, a line of connection between the original events and the developed Catholic Church.

Such was Catholic Modernism. It built upon the idea of development. In so doing, it bore cheerfully a large degree of scepticism about the historical character of the New Testament documents, making a virtue of critical necessity. And it shifted much weight from the importance of the original events to the importance of the religious experience of the Catholic Church. Within the short years of Catholic Modernism before the débâcle, and in the work of its exponents subsequently, there were different strains. Baron von Hügel was with the Modernists in his conviction that historical criticism must be pursued with uncompromising integrity: but he was suspicious of the immanentist doctrine which he sensed in Loisy, and his own religion was rooted in the conviction of divine transcendence. On any shewing, the conflict with Papal authority was inevitable, and the most ruthless condemnation of Modernism was given by Pope Pius X in the decree *Pascendi Gregis*. The drama ended with the tragic spectacles of Tyrrell dying excommunicate and being buried at Storrington, with the Abbé Bremond in the little group of mourners, and of Loisy living to a great old age and moving finally into scepticism.

Outside the Roman Catholic Church, however, the influence of Catholic Modernism made itself felt. The influence varied in its character. In an extreme version it could mean the assigning of supreme authority to the Christian experience, and to the ideas expressed in it—with little concern for history. Frequently it meant a tendency to a pragmatist philosophy (such as was in vogue in the early years of the century) according to which truth was measured by its practical result. Always, it meant an insistence that religious experience is among the primary data

Piety and Freedom

for theology, and this was congruous with the rising interest in mysticism in England.

There were Anglicans who were sensitive to the religious outlook of Catholic Modernism, with its blending of sacramental piety and intellectual freedom; and Tyrrell's writings especially had many Anglican readers. T. A. Lacey, in a now-forgotten book, *The Historic Christ* (1903), made a modified use of Loisy's method. It was in Anglo-Catholic writers that this influence came specially to be felt, in an emphasis upon the significance of Christian experience both for apologetics and for theological construction. We shall see later how, in contrast with Gore's primary emphasis upon history, there grew up a type of liberal Catholic theology wherein the weight put upon experience was equally strong.[1] The most notable of Anglican works which owe much to Catholic Modernism is *Belief and Practice* by Sir Will Spens (1915). In this highly original book Spens argued that theology is the rationalization of Christian religious experience, and, as such, it must, like scientific theory, face the twofold test of (a) explaining the particular facts, and (b) being congruous with a 'general outlook' which is rational. In explaining the data of religious experience in the apostolic age and in the main Christian tradition, the orthodox doctrine of the Incarnation meets this twofold test, whereas both the Liberal Protestant doctrine and the doctrine of a 'diffused incarnation' fail to do so.

It is time, however, to return to the English Modernists, whose story we are to follow. In the main, their kinship was with the Liberal Protestantism of the Continent, not with Catholic Modernism. Dr. Inge on one occasion vehemently disclaimed connection with the latter: 'We are no more desirous of being mixed up with them, than they with us.' But there was a little

---

[1] For an extreme instance, which it would be unfair to take as typical of the author, I would quote this sentence. 'The sacraments are to be interpreted not in the light of their historical origins (about which, in most cases, to be frank, we know surprisingly little) but rather in the light of what they have come to be, and of the part which they have actually played in the life of the Church', *Studies in Historical Christianity* by A. E. J. Rawlinson (1922). Rawlinson's *Dogma, Fact and Experience* (1915) was a significant instance of Catholic Modernist influence upon Anglican thought.

Modernism

more affinity than Inge allows or than has been generally recognized. Both schools drew upon the conception of development, albeit in different ways. There appeared also within English Modernism a strain of pragmatism similar to that of some of the Modernist Catholics: we see this in Percy Gardner's *Modernity and the Churches* (1910), and in Bethune-Baker's *The Faith of the Apostles' Creed* (1918), where the dogmas are expounded as symbols of the Christian moral experience.[1] Still, it was in the main the leading Liberal Protestant assumptions which fashioned the outlook most characteristic, through several decades, of the English 'Modern Churchmen'.

III

The Modernists in England included thinkers as various as they were distinguished. W. R. Inge, Dean of S. Paul's from 1910 to 1935, was a Christian Platonist in the tradition of Whichcote. He had been, notably in his Bampton Lectures of 1899, a pioneer in the revived study of mysticism. If his greatest work is his exposition of the philosophy of Plotinus in two volumes of Gifford Lectures, his most characteristic teaching is to be seen in his two volumes of *Outspoken Essays* and in an essay on the theology of S. John in *Cambridge Biblical Essays*. The mystical element in religion was for him primary, and he believed that the essence of Christian religion was separable from the traditional scheme of dogma and institution; though he was deeply convinced of the importance of the Incarnation and severely critical of attempts to base Christianity on idea rather than on history. Modernism included for him a vehement dislike of the

[1] It is not difficult to see affinity with Catholic Modernism in such a passage as this. 'To dismiss these stories of Christ's miracles, the virginal conception, and the empty tomb as worthless, when we are seeking a true valuation of Jesus and the whole experience of which he was the centre, is to shut one's eyes to some of the bits of evidence we have about him and the impression which he produced. It is not the work of the scientific enquirer to do so. They come to us . . . from the realm of poetry and picture, but the experience of men and women like ourselves underlies them, and they help us to estimate the character and quality of that experience.' Bethune-Baker, *The Way of Modernism*, p. 46.

ptolemaic imagery in the Creed, and he ascribed to traditionally minded Christians a greater literalism about this imagery than they probably entertained. Inge's dislike of institutionalism did not prevent his affinity with great Christian teachers in many ages, and he had a big influence in bringing home the essence of religion to thoughtful people. His famous essay on S. Paul ends with these characteristic words: 'S. Paul understood what most Christians never realize, namely that the Gospel of Christ is not *a* religion, but religion itself, in its most universal and deepest significance.'[1]

Another, and perhaps more typical, leader of liberal Modernism was Hastings Rashdall, Tutor of New College from 1895 to 1917, and Dean of Carlisle from 1917 till his death in 1924. Immensely erudite both as philosopher and historian, Rashdall felt a missionary vocation to liberate the Christian religion from the hindrances which prevented its speedy acceptance by the modern intelligence: archaic dogmas, miracle and the requirements of literalism in clerical subscription. With deep piety, he found himself satisfied by an exclusively 'symbolic' view of the Incarnation and an exclusively 'exemplarist' view of the Atonement. With massive learning, he was ready to shew that modern versions of orthodoxy sometimes involved arbitrary or misleading interpretations of ancient writers, and it was a favourite theme that the orthodoxy of teachers such as Gore presented the doctrine of the Trinity in a manner more tritheistic than S. Augustine or S. Thomas Aquinas would countenance. On the other hand, he was apart from Inge, and nearer to Gore, in a distrust of mysticism and a dislike of the appeal to religious experience.

The Modernists, to their own loss, became a party, though perhaps this was inevitable. Founded in 1898, the Churchmen's Union for the Advancement of Religious Thought was renamed in 1928 the Modern Churchmen's Union. It included, besides the marked individuality of Inge and Rashdall, men who developed a more distinctively self-conscious modernist line with its particular tenets, such as H. D. A. Major, for many years

[1] *Outspoken Essays*, first series, p. 229.

Modernism

Principal of Ripon Hall, and M. G. Glazebrook, first headmaster of Clifton and subsequently Canon of Ely. It was very clear what these liberals desired to liberate the Christian religion *from*. But what was the essence of the theology which they would retain? Most of them would probably say: a belief in Jesus as the revealer of God and in eternal life through Him. Some of them might dwell on an immanentist view of God and the world: others, eschewing philosophy, would dwell upon the historical Jesus, holding that, apart from Him, we do not know God at all. Others held that it was only after liberation from obsolete dogmas that there could begin to be a fresh discovery of Christianity in its meaning for the contemporary world. In short, the Modernists had in common less a distinctive theology or philosophy than a 'platform' of ideals and reforms.

It was not surprising that Charles Gore, both as divine and as disciplinary bishop, felt that the Modernists were challenging things most dear to him and most vital for the integrity of the faith. In the next chapter we shall see the controversies about subscription in which Gore took a leading part. It was amid such controversies that some of the ablest Biblical scholars found themselves among the Modernists, such as William Sanday and B. H. Streeter, their Modernism being less a theological tenet than a plea for the rights of critical scholarship within the Church. Gore, however, was concerned with an issue more fundamental than subscription. He believed that beneath the Modernist rejection of the miraculous there was a distinctive philosophy which, derived from idealism or other types of immanentism, identified the natures of God and Man in such a way as to blur the distinction between Creator and creature. 'This is not a movement which must be satisfied with the elimination from the Creed of certain miracles, leaving the ideas about God and Man untouched. It is a movement which, as a whole, demands a trenchant rehandling of our doctrine of God and Man.'[1]

Was this a correct judgment? Modernism as a whole was too varied for a single formula to describe it. But in so far as certain

[1] *The Reconstruction of Belief*, p. 466.

Christ's Deity

of the leading Modernists, especially Rashdall and Bethune-Baker, disclosed a distinctive Christological theory, it was near to what Gore was describing—with the difference that, for the former, it was idealistic philosophy and, for the latter, it was the concept of evolution which provided the key. Rashdall devoted some pages to Christology in his *Philosophy and Religion* (1909). I quote some words which show the line of thought which, despite the ardent piety which it expressed, contains phrases vulnerable to Gore's criticism.

> We cannot say intelligibly that God dwells in Christ, unless we have already recognized that in a sense God dwells in and reveals Himself in Humanity at large, and in each particular human soul. But I fully recognize that, if that is all that is meant by the expression 'divinity of Christ', that doctrine would be evacuated of nearly all that makes it precious to the hearts of Christian people. And, therefore, it is all-important that we should go on to insist that men do not reveal God equally. The more developed intellect reveals God more completely than that of the child or the savage: and the higher and more developed moral consciousness reveals Him more than the lower, and above all the actually better man reveals God more than the worse man. Now, if in the life, teaching and character of Christ . . . we can discover the highest revelation of the divine nature, we can surely attach a real meaning to the language of the Creeds which singles him out from all the men that ever lived as the one in whom the ideal relation of man to God is most completely realized. If God can only be known as revealed in Humanity, and Christ is the highest representative of Humanity, we can very significantly say 'Christ is the Son of God, very God of very God, of one substance with the Father', though the phrase undoubtedly belongs to a philosophical dialect which we do not habitually use (pp. 180-181).

Deity includes the human race, and the Nicene definition of Christ's deity and the devotion due to Him as divine are justified in virtue of His being the highest representative of humanity.

It was this issue which came to a head in the event, sensational at the time, of the Conference of the Modern Churchmen's Union at Girton College in 1921. The story is worth recalling. The Modernist cause had at the time been somewhat embarrassed by the recent appearance of the first volume of *The*

Beginnings of Christianity, under the Editorship of Foakes-Jackson and Kirsopp Lake. This volume was to be the initiation of a critical and historical examination of Christian origins, with the collaboration of a big team of scholars from America and Europe. But, prematurely perhaps, the Editors included within the first volume their own investigation of the historical traditions concerning Jesus, with results highly inconvenient for the Modernist devotion to the Jesus of history. According to Jackson and Lake, the religion of the apostolic age was a sacramental catholicism; but, when we have pruned away the accretions made by the Early Church, the picture of Jesus which was left was of a figure with an ethical message, prophetic in a mild sense, but extraordinarily jejune: 'the only presentation known to me', wrote C. E. Raven, 'which makes Jesus merely dull'.[1] To the Modernists in general, the essay of Jackson and Lake was a blow and an embarrassment. It caused a certain nervousness to accompany the opening of the Girton Conference, especially as Foakes-Jackson had been included among the readers of the papers. Indeed, his paper proved to be as tiresome as some had feared. 'Lake and I refused to make things easier for liberals by shewing connections between synoptic germs and later liberal concepts. We also refused to make things easier for the sacramentalists. We were convinced that the present time is one in which the Church needs a plainer statement of the difficulties of modern Christianity, that it may realise where it stands.' Dr. H. L. Goudge subsequently described Foakes-Jackson's part in the Conference with some appropriateness as 'an accusing historical conscience'.[2]

The importance of Girton for theological history is the exposition made of a distinctive Modernist doctrine by Rashdall and Bethune-Baker. Their papers are perhaps its classic expression.

Rashdall's subject was 'Christ as Logos and as Son of God'.[3]

---

[1] *The Creator Spirit*, p. 235.   [2] In *Church Quarterly Review*, April 1922.

[3] The paper was reprinted in *Jesus God and Man*, a collection of essays on Christology. Other important papers on the same subject were collected in a posthumous volume, *God and Man*.

God Incarnate

He laid down some essential preliminaries. (1) Jesus did not formally claim Divinity for Himself. (2) Jesus was in fullest sense *a man*. (3) It is untrue that the human soul of Jesus pre-existed. (4) The Virgin Birth is not necessarily implied in the Incarnation, nor (5) the omniscience of Jesus on earth. These propositions were quoted widely in the Press in the days following the Conference, and were supposed to be instances of lamentable heresy. But, so far, there was little about them that was either novel or devastating. The first had been long recognized by moderate critical study; (2) is acceptable, though with caveats against the possibility of a Nestorian interpretation; (3) is orthodox enough, and (5) had been widely accepted since *Lux Mundi*. But why did Rashdall select these particular propositions? We see why when we pass on to the ensuing argument. 'If "divine" and "human" are mutually exclusive terms, then belief in the God-Man is absurd.' 'But all men are reproductions of the divine mind, and in all true human thinking there is a reproduction of divine thought. . . . In the conditions of the highest human life, we have access as nowhere else, to the inmost nature of the divine.' 'Thus, it is impossible to maintain that God is fully incarnate in Christ, and not incarnate at all in anyone else. . . . But not equally in all: against many philosophic critics we maintain the supreme Incarnation in one man.' The Logos conception serves to express this: and if the relation of the Logos to the Father is difficult, let it be remembered, urged Rashdall, that there is no need to follow some of the Fathers who treat the Trinity as three divine minds—a virtual tritheism, for we are free to follow Augustine and Aquinas who, in Rashdall's view, taught three modes of one divine mind or activity.

Bethune-Baker's thesis on 'Jesus as both Human and Divine' was similar. We start by knowing Jesus as Man: only in so doing shall we know Him as God. We must 'absolutely jettison the traditional doctrine that His personality was not human but divine'. 'He did not think of Himself as God. . . . If therefore we are to work with the orthodox theory of the Incarnation, we can only do so by making use of the conception of kenosis to the fullest extent. This is the nearest to us orthodoxy can come. Be content if our friends can get only thus far.' But orthodoxy, even when modified by kenosis, will not serve. The clue is that 'God and Man are indissolubly interrelated: neither is complete without the other. God is being actualized, fulfilled in Man. Man comes to the fulfilment of his potentiality in God.' 'The historic process of human experience is God's own experience.' So the argument moves on to the climax, 'In getting to know Jesus we get to know God . . . but only by knowing Him always as Man. . . . It is not from anything that I know beforehand about God that I infer Jesus as God Incarnate. My concept of God is formed by my conception of Jesus.' [1]

The Girton Conference caused some stir in the Church, and indeed in the country. Reports in the newspapers, quoting phrases out of context, created the impression that Rashdall and others were denying that Christ was divine. Unfair denunciations were made from the orthodox side. Gore himself obscured his own case by vehemence, and just a little unfairness. As a result of a *gravamen* submitted by Darwell Stone and others, the Upper House of the Convocation of Canterbury had a learned debate on the matter, and passed a resolution affirming the Nicene faith ('and in particular concerning the eternal pre-existence of the Son of God, His true Godhead and His Incarna-

---

[1] W. N. Pittenger in *The Word Incarnate* (1959) argues that Bethune-Baker's Christology is of considerable present value (ibid. pp. 198–202, cf. the same author's *Tomorrow's Faith Today*, pp. 47–68). Pittenger is unconvincing in that he has to admit so much recklessness among Bethune-Baker's statements, 'Sometimes indeed Bethune-Baker's terminology seems to suggest rather more of a "point to point" identity than the facts warrant; and when he affirms that the creatures "are the counterparts of God's will and love, as necessary to the existence of God as he is to theirs," we must certainly hesitate.' 'It is dangerous to write as he did that "Jesus becomes for me merged, as it were in God, or identical with God".' 'Bethune-Baker did not always see the danger in what now and again amounted to equating God with the hypostatization of ideals and values.' It does not suffice to excuse 'the defects in Bethune-Baker's Christological approach . . . by the fact that he was a pioneer in this effort to use evolutionary ideas', for the ideas had long been in the field, and Bethune-Baker was a mature, highly trained scholar. His strength was in historical theology: in metaphysics his mind was confused.

Deity and Humanity

tion'), welcoming free inquiry, deprecating the 'mere blunt denunciation of contributions made by earnest men in their endeavour to bring new light' and giving warning against 'the publication of debatable suggestions as if they were ascertained truths' (2 May 1922). The speeches in the debate dealt with particular statements at Girton which had a heterodox ring, but none shewed perception of the main issue, upon which Gore (now in retirement from the see of Oxford) put his finger. That this was the main issue, and that Gore did not misrepresent it, is seen from some candid words of Dr. Major:

> Yet Dr. Gore is correct in affirming that we believe that there is only one substance of the Godhead and the Manhood, and that our conception of the difference between Deity and Humanity is one of degree. The distinction between Creator and creature, upon which Dr. Gore and the older theologians place so much emphasis, seems to us to be a minor distinction. It is like the distinction between omnipotent and non-omnipotent. It is not a moral distinction at all, and we fail to see how one can base an ethical system upon it (*Modern Churchman*, Vol. XI, p. 357, October 1921).

There could be no plainer acknowledgment that Gore had put his finger on the issue. What is strange is Major's failure to perceive it to be an issue at all.[1]

IV

It would, however, be wrong to suppose that the particular philosophy and theology which came to a head in the Girton crisis represented the general mind of the Modernists. We have seen how great was the variety among them. Theirs was a rebellion and an ideal, rather than a system. In an interesting essay,[2] Dr. Vidler has distinguished liberality and liberalism. The first is the temper of free inquiry and intellectual generosity. The second is a particular set of tenets drawn from the Victorian age: the inevitability of social, moral and religious progress, and (we might add) the uniformity of nature as a

---

[1] For another aspect of the controversy between Gore and Rashdall, see Appendix D.
[2] A. R. Vidler, *Essays in Liberality*, 1957, Ch. i.

principle which controls belief about the relation of God, man and the world. Both liberality and liberalism became apparent with the Modernist movement. Liberality shewed itself in the pursuit of a critical investigation and in the practice of an inward, mystical religion marked by a sympathy with every manifestation of the religious spirit. But liberality can never organize itself as a party without contradicting itself and involving itself in a limited set of tenets. In this case the tenets were those of liberalism in the sense in which Vidler uses the word; and they could be the more limiting when they were half-conscious than when they were avowed.

Modernism was an inevitable movement: the self-conscious effort to protect the rights of free inquiry, to use the findings of the modern sciences and to insist that there is development in the understanding of the Christian faith. It receded as a movement, as its virtues were palpably the monopoly of no party, and was diffused here, there and anywhere (though not, of course, everywhere) in the Church. The pursuit of critical studies of the Bible was the monopoly of no one school of thought. And as for effective contact between theology and contemporary thought the two most outstanding instances are perhaps F. R. Tennant's use of the methods of the empirical sciences in his *Philosophical Theology* and Thornton's use of Whitehead's philosophy in his *The Incarnate Lord*: and, of these men, the one might have called himself a Modernist and the other not.

In the avowedly Modernist writings of the period [1] there is much with which theologians of many kinds would concur, much tilting at traditionalist crudities which few would care to defend. Where there is an underlying philosophy it is commonly that of the identity of the natures of God and Man, and where there is an underlying assumption it is commonly that of the uniformity of nature. It was the dominance of this concept which determined much of the Modernist treatment of the

---

[1] As examples from three decades I would cite M. G. Glazebrook, *The Faith of a Modern Churchman* (1918); H. D. A. Major, *English Modernism* (1927); R. D. Richardson, *The Gospel of Modernism* (1933).

Philosophy in Disguise

Bible. While historical criticism professed to be examining the records without presuppositions, it frequently employed the presupposition of the uniformity of nature in judging the evidence concerning events allegedly supernormal. Thus the idea that God does things in particular in history, in mighty acts of redemption and judgment, was excluded. Consequently the Kingdom of God could be identified with the moral and spiritual progress of men striving to do God's will in a world from which God seemed almost excluded. The key to the understanding of the Bible was lost, for just as the miraculous events were incredible, so the imagery of the Bible was largely irrelevant.

So it was that Modernism, claiming to be an impartial science but being in large part a 'philosophy in disguise', began to seem an old-fashioned thing. Some words of E. G. Selwyn deserve to be recalled:

> The gravamen against modernism is not that it seeks for uniformities, but that it postulates for the explanation of Christianity as a whole uniformities which apply only to a particular part of it, and so reduce it to the level of a natural religion. . . . Anglican theology of the last half of the nineteenth century, as seen in *Essays and Reviews* or in *Lux Mundi*, was largely concerned with the attempt to come to terms with current scientific conceptions and to see how far they could be accepted without danger to the Christian faith. What is called Modernism today results from hanging on too long to conceptions then current, and forcing them further than they will go, and its upshot is to reduce Christianity as a living religion to a mere shadow of itself. We might say that Modernism bears the same relation to the theology of today as Haeckel's monism bore to the science of even a generation ago (*Essays Catholic and Critical*. Preface to second edition, 1929).

What was the answer to be? Gore gave it only partly, by shewing with crystal clarity what the issues really were. But he impeded his own answer as a scholar by making appeals to ecclesiastical authority: and he was unable in consequence to meet his opponents on their ground of critical inquiry by their own critical science to the very full. That was the answer which was necessary, and it came to be given in the 'twenties and 'thirties and subsequently, by Biblical science, critical and yet free from arbitrary assumptions. No answer in the long run suffices which does not take historical inquiry with the same seriousness which liberalism had claimed for it. But more than history is involved. Let me continue the quotation from E. G. Selwyn:

> Liberal Catholicism, on the other hand, stands for the new or newly realized facts which give to theology its autonomy as a science. It appeals to those facts of religious experience which, though embedded in history, cannot be adequately accounted for by historical science alone. As against the evolutionary immanentism characteristic of modernist thought, it emphasizes the facts of human freedom and accountability, and the extremes of guilt and non-attainment which cry aloud for the otherness of God and for a redemption that shall come from above; and it points to the Christian experience as the experience of such a redemption centred in Christ.

In a coming lecture we shall see how far Liberal Catholicism was able to achieve that synthesis of faith and criticism where Modernism had failed. But the task is ever with us, for when shall we outgrow the difficulties of the twofold calling: to think and to believe?

CHAPTER SIX

CREED AND SUBSCRIPTION

I

IN the preceding chapter we saw how the Modernist movement in the Church of England was involved in what Gore described as 'a trenchant rehandling of our doctrine of God'. But to practical-minded Englishmen the issues were seen in less metaphysical terms, and the questions prominent in controversy were those which concerned the miraculous events mentioned in the Creed: 'born of the Virgin Mary', 'on the third day he rose again from the dead'. The issue was not simple. There were not only those who held a doctrine which rigorously excluded the miraculous; there were also those who, believing in the Incarnation as a supernatural event, were on grounds of historical criticism hesitant about believing in the particular mode of the Incarnation which the birth narratives in the Gospels of Luke and Matthew describe. There was especially in the first decade of this century a particular vogue of scholarly sensitivity: a feeling that since certain questions were very new, and the scholarly disciplines relevant to them were also very new, suspense of judgment was an obligation. In this mood some scholars were impressed by the fact that the earliest apostolic presentation of Christ as divine Lord and Saviour contained apparently no reference to the Conception by the Virgin Mary, and by the possibility that this story was an accretion to the primitive tradition. Similarly it seemed possible to doubt whether the apostolic faith that Jesus was alive and risen was necessarily bound up with the traditions concerning the raising of the *body* from the tomb.

The controversies on these questions form a chapter in Anglican theological history important in itself, but the more interesting since it involved the fortunes of churchmen as great as Hensley Henson and William Temple. In these controversies there was disclosed the characteristic Anglican temper in dealing with doubt in a time of transition.

This Anglican temper had its critics. We have to ask whether its existence did not serve in the long run both the needs of intellectual integrity and the vindicating of the Catholic faith in its fulness.

Different questions were often entangled: the truth of certain scriptural narratives, the importance of it as a part of the Christian faith, the legitimacy of understanding the corresponding clauses in the Creed in a 'symbolic' sense, the fitness of a man holding ecclesiastical office if he recited the Creed in such a sense. There was also the distinction between an attitude of denial and an attitude of hesitant suspense.

Throughout this controversy Gore was seen as protagonist. His attitude to the question of the Creed was one part of his attitude about the corporate adherence of the Church of England to those limits of orthodoxy and liberty which he held to be fundamental. This attitude was unchanged throughout his episcopate, and it is set out most clearly in a letter to the clergy of the Diocese of Oxford published in 1914 with the title *The Basis of Anglican Fellowship*. Here Gore is seen fighting a disciplinary battle on several fronts, contending equally with the more Roman trends in the Anglo-Catholic movement, with the more lax approach towards intercommunion with the non-episcopal churches, and with the treatment of the Creeds by some of the liberal clergy. If it is with the last of those questions alone that we are here concerned, it is important to see that for Gore it was one of several questions upon which he felt obliged to be firm on a principle of justice on all sides.

Behind Gore the disciplinarian there was always Gore the theologian. He distinguished between clauses in the Creed which describe realities beyond history or human experience, and clauses which refer to events on the plane of history. In the case of the former, e.g. 'he came down from heaven', 'he sitteth at the right hand of God', we must take the phrases to be symbolical. But in the case of the latter, e.g. 'born of the Virgin Mary', 'on the third day he rose again from the dead', only a literal understanding is tolerable. Gore's vehement upholding of this view surprised some who recalled his own rôle as a 'liberal' at the time of *Lux Mundi*. But he himself claimed that it was his own fidelity to the methods of historical criticism which led him to his view. He had concluded on historical grounds that the evidence for both the Virgin Birth and the Resurrection from the tomb on the third day was overwhelmingly strong and that only a dogmatic prejudice against the miraculous could cause anyone to reject it. He felt that this negative prejudice was the enemy, and those who held it were guilty of a disqualifying perversity. To him the issue was of supreme importance because his belief in the love and righteousness of God, a belief tried and tested in the fire of his keen sensitivity to the suffering of the world, was bound up with the vindication of the divine freedom and redemptive power in an intrinsically miraculous Incarnation attested by history. There was no manifestation of divine love in the uniformity of nature.

Over against Gore there stood William Sanday, the Lady Margaret Professor of Divinity in the University of Oxford. Sanday's influence had been, on the whole, conservative, and it was in 1912 that in a discussion at the Oxford society known as the 'Theological Dinner' he disclosed his inability to commit himself to those miracles in the Gospel which were *contra naturam* as well as *supra naturam*. The words in which he later put his view upon one of the questions are worth quoting:

> In regard to the Birth of our Lord I would say that I believe most emphatically in His supernatural Birth; but I cannot so easily bring myself to think that His Birth was (as I should regard it) unnatural. This is just a case where I think the Gospels use symbolical language. I can endorse entirely the substantial meaning of that verse of St. Luke (1 : 35): 'The Holy Ghost shall come upon thee, and the power of the Most High shall overshadow thee: wherefore also that which is to be born shall be called holy and the Son of God.' This is deeply metaphorical and symbolical, and carries us into regions where thought is baffled. I do not doubt that the Birth of our Lord was sanctified in every physical respect in the

most perfect manner conceivable. The coming of the Only-begotten in the world could not but be attended by every circumstance of holiness. Whatever the Virgin Birth can spiritually mean for us is guaranteed by the fact that the Holy Babe was divine. Is it not enough to affirm this with all our heart and soul, and be silent as to anything beyond?[1]

Sanday wrote these words in a pamphlet entitled *Bishop Gore's Challenge to Criticism*, being roused to indignation by Gore's plea that those who held office in the Church while reciting these clauses in a non-literal sense were dishonest and that the Bishops should make a collective affirmation on this issue. To read Sanday's words is to feel at its strongest the case of those whom Gore was denouncing.

Sanday argues that Gore was not facing the bearing of criticism upon the New Testament in the spirit in which he had taught others to face its bearing upon the Old, and that he was drawing his own arbitrary line between what was symbolical and what was historical. The same rejoinder was to be made later with special lucidity by A. E. Taylor in the second volume of his Gifford Lectures: the ancient Church, he points out, would have taken *other* clauses in the Creed, e.g. 'He ascended into heaven', locally and literally, and might have condemned Gore's own concessions to symbolism.

A number of episodes kept the issue in prominence. As Bishop of Worcester, Gore had caused a clergyman named G. E. Beeby to resign his benefice since he distinctly denied the miracles in the Creed. In 1912 the essay by B. H. Streeter on 'The Historic Christ', in the volume *Foundations*,[2] distressed Gore by its treatment of the Resurrection in terms of veridical visions; but Gore held his hand from any disciplinary measure on account of a plea made to him by Scott Holland that the essay contained no dogmatic denial of the supernatural. In 1911 Talbot, as Bishop of Winchester, withdrew the licence of J. M. Thompson, Fellow

[1] *Bishop Gore's Challenge to Criticism* (1914), pp. 19-20.
[2] *Foundations*, which had among its contributors Streeter, Temple and Rawlinson, was important not for any single thesis within it but as an illustration of the effort of some liberal theologians of somewhat different standpoints to meet the problems of the time.

Policies of Repression

and Dean of Divinity at Magdalen College, on account of a book disowning the miraculous in the New Testament.[1] In 1914 Gore was pressing for an affirmation by the Bishops in the Upper House of the Convocation of Canterbury that the acceptance of the historical miracles in the Creed was a necessary part of the meaning of Clerical Subscription. He was vehemently concerned to force the issue as he himself saw it.

It is here that there comes into our story the sagacious ecclesiastical statesman, Archbishop Randall Davidson. Davidson was no theologian. But he knew enough of the modern history of the Church to realize that orthodoxy can injure itself by policies of repression, and enough of human nature to realize that a Declaration such as Gore desired would drive into negative positions some of those who asked for no more than a right to suspend judgment on certain historical questions. Furthermore, Davidson had been influenced by a small but weighty book by Armitage Robinson (Dean of Westminster, 1902–1911, and of Wells, 1911–1933) entitled *Some Thoughts on the Incarnation* (1903). This book deserves to be recalled as a little gem of Anglican theology. Written with keen sensitiveness to those who felt difficulty about the Virgin Birth, this essay draws out the place of the Incarnation as intrinsically miraculous in relation to man and nature, and shews how belief in the Virgin Birth is at once subordinate and congruous. But the book contains also an open letter to the Archbishop deprecating the handling by episcopal declarations of a matter best dealt with by scholar meeting scholar on his own ground. It is a singularly lucid piece of exposition and persuasion, and Archbishop Davidson was to refer to it on several occasions of distress in the Church.

Encouraged by Armitage Robinson's thesis, and assisted by Dr. F. H. Chase, the Bishop of Ely, a Cambridge scholar versed in the academic work of historical criticism, Davidson was able to steer the Bishops away from the resolution desired by Gore, which called for mention of the Virgin Birth and the Bodily

[1] J. M. Thompson, *Miracles in the New Testament*, 1911. Cf. also his *Through Facts to Faith*, 1912, and an appreciation by W. N. Pittenger in *Anglican Theological Review*, October 1957.

Resurrection as 'essential parts of the faith of the Church' and for the censure of a symbolic interpretation as 'seriously contrary to sincerity of profession'. Instead, he secured the passing by the Upper House of the Convocation of Canterbury of a Resolution which deserves for its historic importance to be quoted in full. It ran thus:

> Inasmuch as there is reason to believe that the minds of many members of the Church of England are perplexed and disquieted at the present time in regard to certain questions of Faith and of Church order, the Bishops of the Upper House of the Province of Canterbury feel it to be their duty to put forth the following Resolutions:
>
> (1) We call attention to the Resolution which was passed in this House on 10 May, 1905, as follows: 'that this house is resolved to maintain unimpaired the Catholic Faith in the Holy Trinity and the Incarnation as contained in the Apostles' and Nicene Creeds, and in the *Quicunque Vult*, and regards the faith there presented, both in statements of doctrine and in statements of fact, as the necessary basis on which the teaching of the Church reposes.'
>
> We further desire to direct attention afresh to the following Resolution which was unanimously agreed to by the Bishops of the Anglican Communion attending the Lambeth Conference of 1908.
>
> 'This Conference, in view of tendencies widely shown in the writings of the present day, hereby place on record its conviction that the historical facts stated in the Creed are an essential part of the Faith of the Church.'
>
> (2) These Resolutions we desire solemnly to reaffirm, and in accordance therewith to express our deliberate judgement that the denial of any of the historical facts in the Creeds goes beyond the limits of legitimate interpretation, and gravely imperils that sincerity of profession which is incumbent on the ministers of the Word and Sacraments. At the same time, recognizing that our generation is called to face new problems raised by historical criticism, we are anxious not to lay unnecessary burdens upon consciences, nor unduly to limit freedom of thought and inquiry, whether among clergy or among laity: We desire, therefore, to lay stress on the need of consideration in dealing with that which is tentative and provisional in the thought and work of earnest and reverent students (Convocation of Canterbury, April 29, 1914).

Gore, though he had not obtained all that he wanted, was fairly content with this Resolution. It stands as an affirmation

The Subscription Controversies

of orthodoxy typically Anglican in form and temper. It affirms the faith of the Church, as Gore himself affirmed it: and it calls for the utmost consideration towards students. Since, however, every teacher in the Church must needs be a student with a student's integrity, the Resolution did not answer all the questions which were to arise about the position of certain individuals and about the attitude of the Church towards them. There were within the period under review two significant personal episodes: those of Hensley Henson and William Temple.

II

The controversies about subscription in the second decade of the century reached a climax in the episode of Hensley Henson and the see of Hereford. Henson, formerly a Fellow of All Souls and Vicar of Barking, was Canon of Westminster and Rector of S. Margaret's from 1900 to 1913, when he became Dean of Durham. Refusing Asquith's offer of the Chair of Ecclesiastical History at Oxford in 1908, Henson had devoted himself to a ministry of preaching widely influential through his liberality of outlook. Hostile to Anglo-Catholicism, staunch in defence of establishment, devoted to the older writers of classical Anglican divinity, Henson regarded himself less as a Modernist than as a 'latitude man who had strayed from the seventeenth century into the twentieth'. In lucid English prose Henson expounded such themes as the religious value of the critical view of the Bible, the non-necessity of particular ecclesiastical polities—with the corollary of intercommunion with all Protestant Churches, the separability of the faith of the Incarnation from its accompanying miracles, and the Lordship of Jesus to be worshipped as divine. Henson was not himself a deep theologian. But with a scholarly concern about the questions of historical inquiry, he did not explicitly deny the miracles mentioned in the Creed, but he tried to cast a protecting mantle over those who did—using speech which was commonly provocative and occasionally reckless.

Creed and Subscription

Trouble arose when, in November 1917, Lloyd George nominated Henson to the see of Hereford.[1] Gore at once took the field, urging the Archbishop that Henson should not be consecrated, as 'he falls outside the limits of tolerable conformity as recognized in our recent declaration in Convocation'. Archbishop Davidson was perturbed as to his course, being ready to examine the facts objectively, and if they called for a refusal to consecrate Henson, he steeled himself for that possibility, carrying as it did the probable corollary of his own resignation. His confidence, however, in Henson's essential orthodoxy as an ardent believer in the Incarnation kept him optimistic. But the skies darkened as a result of two letters to *The Times*. One was from Darwell Stone, citing some of Henson's heterodox utterances. The other was from Sanday, who assumed (wrongly) the identity of Henson's view with his own and expounded the modernist thesis that the miracles mentioned in the Creed were 'realistic expressions, adopted to the thought of the time, of ineffable truths which the thought of the time could not express in any other way'—a philosophic view somewhat removed from Henson's own mode of thought and expression. Henson was unwilling to appease the situation by publishing explanations and retractations. Finally, the Archbishop, feeling completely in a deadlock, got Henson, most reluctantly, to write an agreed answer to a letter of his own—though Henson insisted on adding its final sentence:

Jan. 16th, 1918.

My dear Henson,

I am receiving communications from many earnest men of different schools who are disquieted by what they have been led to suppose to be your disbelief in the Apostles' Creed, and especially the clauses relating to our Lord's birth and Resurrection. I reply to them that they are misinformed, and that I am

---

[1] The chief sources for the Hereford episode are G. K. A. Bell, *Randall Davidson*, H. H. Henson, *Retrospect of an Unimportant Life*, Vol. I, and F. L. Cross, *Darwell Stone*. None of these accounts made use of the letters of Hensley Henson now available, and the use of these in my text may remove misunderstandings which have hitherto existed.

Miracles in the Creed

persuaded that when you repeat the words of the Creed you do so *ex animo* and without any desire to change them. I think I understand your reluctance to make at this moment a statement the motives of which might be misconstrued, and it is only because you would relieve many good people from real distress that I ask you to let me publish this letter with a word of reassurance from yourself.

Randall Cantuar:

Jan. 17th, 1918.

My dear Lord Archbishop,

I do not like to leave any letter of yours unanswered. It is strange that it should be thought by anyone to be necessary that I should give such an assurance as you mention, but of course what you say is absolutely true. I am indeed astonished that any candid reader of my published books, or anyone acquainted with my public ministry of thirty years, could entertain a suggestion so dishonourable to me as a man and as a clergyman.

H. HENSLEY HENSON.

The skies cleared. Gore withdrew his protest. 'I consider myself now entitled to declare that Dr. Henson believes what I thought he disbelieved, and affirms *ex animo* what I thought he did not affirm.' Some other High Churchmen, such as Darwell Stone and Fr. Puller, S.S.J.E., were still dissatisfied, in that there was no explicit repudiation by Henson of statements doubting the miracles in the Creeds. What did Henson himself mean? In the light of evidence now available from Henson's subsequent diaries and letters it is quite clear (as it was clear at the time to Darwell Stone) that Henson meant neither to make any sort of recantation nor to affirm that he had believed in the miracles in the Creed. He meant that he had always believed, and still believed, in the Creed *ex animo*: and 'I assumed that every considering and educated person understood by an *ex animo* acceptance of the Creed an acceptance which was deliberate and sincere, not an acceptance which was nakedly and unintelligently literal' (*Retrospect of an Unimportant Life*, I, p. 214). This was consistent with what Henson had written some years previously in *Sincerity and Subscription*. 'The clause in the Creed must be supposed to affirm the two truths about our Lord on which the Apostles in their writing lay emphasis, His true manhood and His essential Deity' (p. 45). Years later Henson was to write to O. C. Quick in a letter thanking him for the gift of his book on *The Doctrines of the Creed*: 'You know already that on the subject of the "Virgin Birth" I am an agnostic, while affirming *ex animo* the Creed in what I believe to be its essential meaning' (*More Letters of H.H.H.*, p. 130).

Henson went to his consecration with a heart wounded by the controversy, thereafter to fulfil at Hereford a happy and much-loved pastoral ministry, and then after two and a half years to be translated to become one of Durham's greatest bishops. In his early years as Bishop of Durham, Henson drew apart from the Modernist movement. The diary of Dean Inge contains some caustic references to this alienation. No one who knew Henson intimately could for a moment accept the explanation that high office gave him conventionality and conservatism or caused him to 'trim': his character and actions through the subsequent years suffice to show the absurdity of such a theory. On this issue he remained unconvinced about the miracles and their necessity to the Incarnation, and he remained also a sincere worshipper of the divine Christ. It was the latter conviction which caused him to take alarm at the time of the Girton Conference in 1921, and it was then that the breach began.

Henson was one of those to whom Modernism had meant liberality and the rights of the scholar to his integrity. He had not reckoned with an attempt at a drastic reconstruction of the Christian faith, still less with one which seemed to obscure the place of 'the Founder'. Girton alarmed him both by the jejune view of Christ propounded by Lake and Foakes-Jackson, and by the philosophy of Rashdall and Bethune-Baker, who seemed to him to maintain Christ's deity only by deifying mankind and blurring the line between Creator and creature. Not for the first or last time in his courageous life, Henson 'burnt his boats'. He writes to his old friend Alfred Fawkes, once a Roman Catho-

The Lordship of Christ

lic and subsequently an Anglican clergyman of the broad school:

> I think it will be worth while to remind these very cocksure modernists that they are in danger (1) of belittling the actual hold of traditional theology on the Christian public, (2) of belittling the scale and perplexity of the 'reconstruction' to which they address themselves, (3) of forgetting that a church cannot proceed on the principles which may fitly control the procedure of a university, (4) that it is an obligation of charity to make sure that the faith of the simple is not gratuitously disturbed.
>
> Finally, tell them to remember that Christianity is Christ's Religion and cannot survive any handling of the Founder which removes Him from the kind of supremacy which He has ever held. *No* version of Christian theology which does not present the proportions and essential contents of apostolic Christianity as disclosed in the New Testament can serve the turn of the modern Church. Kirsopp Lake and Foakes-Jackson have drifted into a position towards Christ which no convert in any age could adopt. It is external, patronising, profane. People feel this: and only feel it the more since they cannot see always how to justify the feeling (H.H.H. to Alfred Fawkes, 23 August 1921).

I quote this letter, which has not previously been published, on account of its personal interest. Henson was of course being unfair in taking Jackson and Lake to be typical. The letter shews that while he was not a deep theologian, he was a man swayed by his heart—and at heart he had a deep consistent devotion to the divine Christ. This had not prevented his championing of historical criticism: but it now estranged him from what he felt to be sophisticated theological constructions inconsistent with what his heart told him. He took up his parable again in a sermon on the Lordship of Christ at the Church Congress in the same year: 'Of the many strange things said at the Modern Churchman's Conference last August, perhaps the strangest on the lips of a Christian minister was the description of the prayer for divine mercy in the litany as the "cringing of a slave". I cannot believe that on reflection any considering Christian man will approve the attitude of mind which such language discloses. Christ's religion is a message of salvation to a sinful and undone race' (*Church and Parson in England*, p. 25).

III

It was not until some years after the Hereford episode that it came to be generally known from the biography of William Temple that he too had been involved personally in the problem of subscription. When he was a young Fellow of Queen's College, Oxford, he had approached Bishop Paget about being ordained, and the question of his attitude to the Creed came under scrutiny. He was able to say, 'I am inclined very tentatively to accept the doctrine of the Virgin Birth and, with rather more confidence, that of the Bodily Resurrection of our Lord', adding subsequently, 'I am very conscious that my opinions are still subject to considerable change. In the statements I sent I stated definitely conclusions to which I am led by very slight preponderance of argument in some cases.' The Bishop concluded that he could not accept to be a commissioned teacher of the Church 'one who in regard to those two main points of history which I believe to be inextricable from our Creed, stands on such uncertain, precarious, unsteady, ground'.

Was ordination to be impossible for William Temple? 'I do not question', he wrote to a friend a few days after the rejection, 'the rightness of the decision, though it is a great disappointment to me.' And, a few days later: 'I am forced, at present at any rate, to emphasize "tentatively" rather than "assent", for as my practical aim in life is to be theoretical, I cannot close a theoretically open question for practical purposes.' But two years later the matter of ordination was reopened, this time between Temple and Archbishop Davidson. Davidson handled the question less in terms of the definition of Temple's position than in terms of the tendency in his mind and the signs of its movement. He elicited that on the Virgin Birth, Temple was in harmony with Armitage Robinson's position in his *Some Thoughts on the Incarnation* and that on the Resurrection 'he could explain neither Christianity nor European history if he did not firmly believe that our Lord was in visible, tangible, personal contact with the disciples as teacher and guide after

His death and Resurrection, and he regards the evidence in favour of what you and I believe true as being in his judgment far stronger than the difficulties, which beset it'. 'I myself regard him', added Davidson in his letter to Bishop Paget, 'as being, in all essential particulars, an orthodox believer both in the Virgin Birth of our Blessed Lord and in His Resurrection. I do not say that he expresses himself respecting either truth with the distinctness (at least as to detail) which has been usual in orthodox theology. But I can see no adequate reason why he should not now be ordained.' [1]

William Temple was therefore ordained by Archbishop Davidson with Bishop Paget's own goodwill. In later years his hesitancy about the Virgin Birth gave place to a very clear conviction as to its historical truth and its congruity with the Incarnation. Indeed 'miracle' could not have been more integrated than it was with the whole structure of Temple's theology, inasmuch as he treated it not only as the vindication of divine transcendence but also the expression of the 'variableness' in nature belonging to the operation of God immanent (cf. *Nature, Man and God*, pp. 287, 294–295). Temple was accustomed in his popular teaching to say: 'To believe in miracle is to take divine personality in deadly earnest.'

It is therefore a memorable fact of Anglican history that it fell to Randall Davidson to decide whether Hensley Henson might become a bishop and whether William Temple might become a priest. A negative decision would have deprived the Church in the one case of one of its greatest bishops and withal a very powerful preacher of faith in the divine Christ, and in the other case of one who was to become foremost in the exposition of orthodoxy with the credal miracles as part and parcel of the whole. Together the two episodes disclose the Anglican vocation—to risk untidiness and rough edges and apparently insecure fences so that it may be in and through the intellectual turmoil of the time—and not in aloofness from it—that the Church teaches the Catholic faith.

---

[1] The story briefly summarized in this paragraph is told fully in Iremonger, *William Temple*, Ch. vii.

Creed and Subscription

An echo of these controversies was to be heard in the Report of the Archbishops' Commission on *Doctrine in the Church of England*, published in 1937. This Report was not designed to say what was lawful within the Church: questions of subscription and discipline were not within its terms of reference. It was no more than a *speculum* of the various views held by theologians at the time. Liberal theology was amply represented. The Report records the view of traditional orthodoxy that the Virgin Birth is congruous with the rôle of Christ as the head of a new humanity and with the supernatural character of the Incarnation; and it records that 'many of us hold, accordingly, that belief in the Word-made-flesh is integrally bound up with belief in the Virgin Birth and that this will increasingly be recognized'. But it also records the presence among the Commission of those 'who hold that a full belief in the Incarnation is more consistent with the supposition that our Lord's birth took place under the normal conditions of human generation'.

It was noticed with interest at the time that this passage showed the existence within the Church of theologians who, believing in the Incarnation, rejected the miraculous conception. But neither this fact nor the fact that Archbishop Temple in his preface to the Report affirmed his own belief in the miracles of the Creed is in the perspective of history so significant as is another fact. It is this: that while in the treatment of the Incarnation in the Report it is allowed that it is legitimate to approach the doctrine from either the Alexandrine or the Antiochene standpoints or their modern equivalents, there is within this comprehensive *speculum* of contemporary Anglican teaching no place whatever for that view of Deity and Manhood which in the hands of Rashdall and Bethune-Baker had loomed so large in the Modernism of two decades earlier. It found no expression at all. The 'trenchant rehandling' of which Gore used to speak had not prevailed. It was no longer in view. That is the supremely significant fact.

Gore had been right in his diagnosis of a doctrine encroaching which was radically different from the historic faith concerning the relation of God the creator and man the creature in His own

Fact and Symbol

image. He had been wrong in ascribing all hesitancy about miracle to that doctrine, and wrong in his demand for measures of exclusion. More rigorous authoritative measures might have excluded Temple from the priesthood and Henson from the episcopate, and driven sensitive historical critics into positions of negation. As it is, theology did her own work, and the 'trenchant rehandling' did not advance, but instead receded. The questions so violently debated have become less prominent. While liberal Modernism has greatly declined, it is perceived that the distinction between fact and symbol in Christian origins cannot be determined with the entire precision which Gore employed, and there is less of a spirit of nervousness about the hesitancies on particular clauses of churchmen whose adherence to the structure of orthodoxy as a whole is certain. A little untidiness is the price which the Church can bear to pay for its power to present the one Catholic faith with sensitiveness to the difficulties of an age.

CHAPTER SEVEN

LIBERAL CATHOLICISM

I

THE Great War of 1914 to 1918 brought its own tale of intellectual and religious unrest. Some of those who were facing the difficulties of faith and doubt in that period have left on record their sense of a theological gap. If Modernism failed to meet their deepest needs, orthodoxy had scarcely found an idiom in which to speak to them. Much water had passed under the bridges since *Lux Mundi*. The task then undertaken needed to be renewed if men were to find a supernatural faith presented with sympathy to the perplexities of the day.

In July 1919 Charles Gore resigned the see of Oxford at the age of sixty-eight, partly on account of his exasperation with certain trends in the policy of the Church (he objected vehemently to Baptism, and not Confirmation, being made the qualification for the lay-electorate under the Enabling Act), and partly through a longing to give his last years to theological writing. 'I have a passion to write.' There followed twelve years, with a literary output remarkable in the crowded life of an old man in demand as a preacher and a spiritual guide.

Gore in this last period found himself somewhat isolated, in spite of the great influence which he still exerted. New Testament criticism had entered a phase more radical than that in which he was at home, and he was wont to argue with impatient vehemence on behalf of particular positions such as the Johannine authorship of the Fourth Gospel. On the other hand, the Catholic Movement in the Church of England had, for many of its adherents, moved beyond the lines which Gore had drawn as its guide and counsellor in earlier years. There was a degree of sympathy for Counter-Reformation piety and devo-

Faith and Practice

tional practice impossible for Gore's strict adherence to antiquity for the rule of faith and to the Book of Common Prayer for the rule of practice. Furthermore, in the years of Gore's episcopate his character as thinker and theologian (always present in its integrity) had been somewhat obscured by his rôle as disciplinarian and defender of the faith. Controversy had tired and exasperated him. It took time for him to shed the impatience of the advocate and to recover the freedom and serenity of the thinker.

I quote a personal impression of Gore from one who had known him in the last years.

> He was then living at No. 6, Margaret Street, and I shall never forget the embrace of that truly numinous figure which thrust me out into the dusk late one November night. . . . It is sometimes said that Gore's mind did not develop after the crisis in his thought represented by *Lux Mundi*. If by this is meant that he was not aware of, or had not tried to come to terms with, most of the best that had been said or written in the relevant fields since then, it seems to me clearly untrue. He was a systematic and astonishingly rapid reader, carefully noting all the more important books. And he had friends of every age and profession into whose intellectual interests he entered with inexhaustible zest. To disagree with an author without being able to say why was a source of mental distress to him, and he spoke gleefully more than once of the satisfaction of disagreeing and, at the same time, of seeing clearly the grounds for disagreement. On the other hand, if the statement means that by the time *Lux Mundi* came to be published he had adopted principles which he retained substantially unaltered for the rest of his life, it seems to me to contain much truth. I sometimes felt that to explain certain characteristic positions it was necessary to go back behind the immediate arguments to earlier mental habits. It was as if the intense conflict of those early days in Oxford had left its mark on a sensitive and highly strung nature, so that his mind latterly tended to run into fixed gladiatorial attitudes suitable, let us say, to a battle with a traditionalist, an encounter with a Darwinian, a deadly grappling with a Papist, and so on. He had been fighting so intensely and on so many different fronts that the alignments almost became established frontiers (J. Conway Davies, *Theology*, November 1932).

There was first the trilogy on *The Reconstruction of Belief*. The first of the volumes, *Belief in God* (1921), is masterly in its moral appeal and its presentation of the claim for the Hebrew prophets as inexplicable except as bearers of divine revelation, but petulant in its treatment of New Testament evidences, to which a disproportionate space is given. In *Belief in Christ* (1922), serenity grows; and in the third volume, *The Holy Spirit and the Church* (1925), the power that was in Gore's earliest writings has returned, making it a classic exposition of the Anglican appeal to Scripture, tradition and reason. Then in a summary volume, *Can we then Believe?* (1926), there comes an essay on Religion, Philosophy and Theology which lays bare with great lucidity Gore's own intellectual procedure; and the Gifford Lectures on *The Philosophy of the Good Life* never depart from the spirit of the sentence 'I am standing before you simply as one rational being speaking to other rational beings, and giving my reasons for holding that the Christian view of the world is the most rational view which we men can entertain'. Gore surveys the conceptions of the good life taught by some of the outstanding moral teachers of mankind, pleading as usual for the *a posteriori* method as superior in philosophy to the *a priori* one. The story represented by Zarathustra, Confucius, Mohammed, Socrates, Plato, the Hebrew prophets and Jesus Christ, forces us to notice a widespread testimony to the supremacy of the good; and the upshot of the story is the twin phenomena of (*a*) the 'idealism' of which Plato is the most mature exponent, and (*b*) the ethical monotheism of the prophets and Jesus Christ. Both phenomena have 'held their own' as instruments of moral progress, and are together intelligible on the basis of the postulates of Christian theism, which is in turn submitted to the test of rationality.

These books are a remarkable story of intellectual growth in the last twelve years of an active life, though it is a growth in the clarification of thought long stored in a deep and restless mind. And these books were not all. There was the summing up of Gore's social teaching in the Holland Lectures on *Christ and Society*. There was the volume, *Jesus of Nazareth*, in the Home University Library. There was the general Editorship of *A New Commentary on Holy Scripture* (1928), a final monument of the

Prophetic Teaching

conservatively critical scholarship of which *Lux Mundi* had been the harbinger some forty years before.

II

Gore as a philosopher was always wont to distinguish philosophy which followed *a priori* reasoning, and philosophy which based itself inductively upon the facts of experience. To him, the supremely important facts of experience were man's possession of free will and the phenomenon of conscience with its majestic, imperative claim. Gore distrusted the distinctive appeal to 'religious experience' such as mysticism. The experience which mattered for him was the moral experience of mankind as a whole.

Such, therefore, are the data for philosophy. They point to ethical theism, with an intrinsic likelihood of revelation if God be personal. Then, the specific phenomenon of the Hebrew prophets needs to be taken into account: a phenomenon upon which, especially in his *Belief in God*, Gore puts immense weight as being inexplicable except in terms of the prophets' own claim: 'Thus saith the Lord.' Then, convinced that the prophetic teaching is divine revelation, we can approach the evidence for the Gospel history. This evidence concerns events, and it is overwhelmingly strong, unless there be an *a priori* prejudice against miracle. Without such prejudice, the events stand demonstrated by historical canons; and, since they are demonstrated, the only reasonable interpretation of them is in terms of Christ's own claim. Such, then, is the reconstruction of belief. First philosophy, as the summary of moral experience, leads us to the rudiments of theism. Then a fair appeal to history shews that revelation has happened. Finally, theology describes and interprets what has been revealed.

Now, putting on one side the question whether Gore's particular historical criticism was adequate or inadequate, we need to consider the larger question of the place of history in the theological scheme. To Gore's critics, he was treating history in the light of a set of assumptions, and consequently not treating

Liberal Catholicism

it with unfettered scientific method. Gore could retort that it was his critics, historians more liberal than himself, who were making assumptions in their treatment of the records. Indeed, the avowedly historical method of liberal scholars was to start with the record of the life of Christ, to examine it with historical science and then to judge as to its value and significance. In doing this they could be unconscious of any philosophical assumptions, but it was quite inevitable that they should have *some*—both in their treatment of evidence in connection with 'abnormal' events and in their criteria for value and appreciation. It is now possible to see that both Gore and his critics were at fault in claiming that they were offering 'just history', and in thinking that 'just history' can provide a basis upon which 'interpretation' can then be brought as a second stage. It is significant, and not without a touch of ironic humour, that those today who see 'history' and 'interpretation' less in isolated compartments would regard both Gore and Lake or Bousset as equally sharing in the same error.

Gore may thus be criticized for putting so much upon history as bare event. It cannot have been that the disciples of Jesus first saw the events as history, and then drew their conclusions; and that cannot quite be our own procedure either. The disciples would hardly know, for instance, of the Resurrection as a proved event apart from knowing the risen Christ's impact upon themselves as now 'raised together with Him'. They would hardly know the facts about Christ apart from the moral regeneration and the spiritual illumination which the facts created, and wherewith they understood the facts. It is therefore impossible to state the historical evidence for Christ without considering the experience of His followers in all its aspects. When this is done, two things seem to be involved: (1) it is necessary to examine the nature and quality of religious experience as among the primary data; (2) though the basis of historical fact for the Christian faith is utterly vital, it is not possible to draw the line between what is history and what is symbol with all the precision and assurance which Gore claimed.

'Religion of the Spirit'

It was on these issues that A. E. Taylor was to criticize Gore's position in his own Gifford Lectures (cf. pp. 108-109 of the present work), and that the younger school of liberal Catholic theologians was to go beyond the lines which Gore had drawn. This school had, before the end of Gore's life, begun to question the validity of Gore's almost purely 'historical' approach, and to urge that it needed to be supplemented by an 'analytical' approach which began with the consideration of the validity of experience. Gore himself was more aware of these needs when he came to write *Can we then Believe?* 'I would have you realize', he says, 'that historical evidence is never demonstrative' (p. 95). In the same book he writes warmly of the mystical element in religion, which he finds to be very important within the Bible itself. But in his Gifford Lectures he finally renewed his distrust of the argument from religious experience as it was commonly made (pp. 313-314).

III

Revelation requires interpretation, and interpretation is guided by divine Authority within the Church. 'Here are three supports, no one of which is sufficient by itself: the Bible, the Church, the individual mind and conscience.' This is the theme of the third volume of Gore's trilogy, *The Holy Spirit and the Church*.

The contemporary world of the nineteen-twenties was full of what was popularly called 'the religion of the Spirit'. This was a belief in a diffused activity of spirit, with no finality of revelation, with sometimes an opposition between the spiritual and the material. Gore contrasts with this popular conception the Biblical doctrine of spirit as a particular and supernatural divine activity, with the Messiah and the Church as the climax. Gore was emphatic that this doctrine does not override the reality of natural religion; he ever pleaded for natural religion against transcendentalist theologies. But as sin has defiled the image of God in man, the revelation of Spirit comes as an urgent summons to salvation, bidding men to 'burn what they

Liberal Catholicism

have adored'. Spirit is finally revealed as the Holy Spirit of Jesus, with the Church as the particular sphere of His activity, inasmuch as it is in fellowship that men are to find the fullness of spiritual life, and it is through the fellowship specifically created by His messianic work that Christ proposes to bring the human race into that fullness.

But how is Authority mediated in the Church? Here Gore characteristically dwells upon the moral nature of authority. It appeals to the conscience. Whenever God speaks to man, the response which is demanded is a moral one. So Christ, when He spoke with divine authority, taught in such a way as to elicit the judgment and moral reflection of the disciples, generating questions in their minds, and helping them to find for themselves the right answer. 'Both S. John and S. Paul seem to have a robust confidence that the good man will come to a right conclusion.' Gore finds in the Church of the Fathers a tone and temper of authority still akin to that of Christ and the apostles: 'an authority which seeks to stimulate and guide, not to deny or suppress the judgment of the mass of churchmen'. Not seldom, the orthodox instinct of the rank and file preserved the faith against false speculations: and a substantial variety of vigorous thought was embraced within the Church's toleration. It was a new and false note struck when Tertullian wrote: 'All the delay of seeking and finding thou hast ended by believing.'

Yet it was a coherent faith which the Church authoritatively taught. The apostolic tradition embodied it, and the Church recognized Holy Scripture as the supreme authority as to what this apostolic tradition is. But Holy Scripture is not in a vacuum. It needs interpretation, and the Church's tradition is the source of that interpretation. This is found in the inspired general mind of the Church, seen in what is taught and believed, *semper, ubique, ab omnibus*. This general mind is particularly declared in the Creeds, congruous as they are in every phrase with scriptural teaching, and in the decisions of the oecumenical councils. 'The authority of the oecumenical councils has a pre-eminence, because there a particular doctrine, which had already agitated the Church and been very fully discussed, was brought into

Divine Authority

distinct light, and the collective mind of the Church was brought to bear upon it, in a sense which gives their decisions an importance and precision which uncontested tradition cannot quite reach.'[1] Gore was accused by some critics of, in some respects, erecting tradition to a position coequal with Scripture. The Nicene Creed was to him certainly as an inviolable, inspired statement. But its congruity with Scripture seemed to him in no doubt. Doctrines and practices of universal acceptance in the early and undivided Church were for Gore *de fide*, if the test of congruity with scriptural truth was assured. The 'Communion of Saints' affords an instance of his method. The belief in the value of mutual prayer between the living and the departed in Christ was generally accepted in the ancient Church: it is congruous with the Biblical teaching of the Church as One Body: it is therefore 'of the faith'. On the other hand, the Invocation of Saints was not universally accepted in pre-Nicene times: it is not therefore 'of the faith': and certain developments of it may impugn the Biblical doctrine of Christ's one mediatorship. Such are the lines of Gore's account of the appeal to Scripture and tradition.

In contrast with the patristic conception of Authority was the conception which came to be characteristic of Roman Catholicism. Gore felt that a peremptory authority of *ecclesia docens* came to replace the moral authority of the primitive conception. 'Tradition' takes on a new meaning, that of ecclesiastical doctrines unknown to Scripture and antiquity, and in effect an addition to the authoritative credenda binding on the faithful. Examining in detail Newman's exposition of Development, Gore lays down the criteria of true development, that it must be open, accessible to the faithful at every stage, and susceptible of appeal to antiquity and Scripture by sound historical scholarship. In making this appeal, the Church today is without an infallible voice. Divine authority has no infallible earthly media. Denying that this is a loss to the Christian, Gore speaks of 'the disposition which craves simply for an authoritative voice, and wants in passive acceptance to get rid of all personal

[1] *The Reconstruction of Belief*, p. 938.

responsibility for the truth', and says, 'I fancy this kind of spirit would have found our Lord a great trial when He was on earth, shewing such reserve in providing plain answers to plain questions and leaving His would-be disciples so much to do for themselves.' Gore was not dismayed by the criticism of his position often made by both Roman Catholic and Protestant critics, who asked where in a divided Christendom the authority of tradition was to be found. Gore believed that an honest investigation of the ancient Church gave clear answers as to what the Catholic faith was and as to how its congruity with Scripture was to be tested.

Based upon the authority of Scripture interpreted by tradition, the Catholic faith, Gore insists, commends itself by its own rational coherence and by its congruity with the known facts about the world which science and man's moral experience have discovered. If the Catholic faith has its own inner coherence, so too has the modernist version of Christianity; given its assumptions, its elements cohere together, but its assumptions do not agree with the experience of humanity in its need of supernatural salvation. As he was wont, Gore asked his readers to test his case by reason at every point.

Gore called the presentation of the faith which he favoured, 'Liberal Catholicism'. It was a favourite phrase. By 'Catholicism' he meant 'that way of regarding Christianity which would see in it not merely or primarily a doctrine of salvation to be apprehended by individuals, but the establishment of a visible society as the one divinely constituted home of the great salvation, held together not only by the inward Spirit but also by certain manifest and external institutions'.[1] This was indeed nothing less than the true character of primitive Christianity. But in view of developments of false kinds of ecclesiastical authoritarianism in history, Gore dwelt on the necessity of a *Liberal* Catholicism'. By this he meant that the belief in the Catholic Church must go hand in hand with the constant appeal to Scripture as the standard of doctrine and moral judgment (the two are inseparable in importance) and the constant

[1] *Catholicism and Roman Catholicism*, p. 1.

concern for the intellectual integrity of the individual. 'Liberal Catholicism' was, Gore believed, precisely embodied in the Anglican appeal to Scripture, antiquity and reason. The favourite term did not mean for Gore a party, or a type of religion, or a particular set of tenets. It was for him virtually synonymous with Anglicanism as rightly understood, for the Church of England in its inherent character appeals to Scripture and tradition and reason, and thus bears witness to the Holy Catholic Church of Christ in a way in which Rome (through its errors) cannot, and the East (through its intellectual conservatism) does not. It was a witness all too often obscured by compromises, and tremendous in its moral demands, yet embodied in the Anglican vocation from the first.

IV

Before Gore's death in 1932 the changes in the intellectual and religious climate had made him seem old-fashioned, even within the movements which he had served and led. Criticism demanded more radical questions and answers. The Catholic Movement looked to less restricted sources of authority, ready to draw at will upon the devotional experience of nineteen centuries of West and East. A new version of Liberal Catholicism appeared. It included more radicalism in Biblical studies, more consideration of the place of experience in theology, and sometimes (though not invariably) more tendencies towards Latin ways of worship. With these tendencies the meaning of the term 'Liberal Catholicism' somewhat shifted. It meant less the Anglican appeal as such than an appeal to a particular synthesis of religion and contemporary scholarship: less an appeal to Catholicism as the institution of the undivided Church than an appeal to Catholicism as the phenomenon of sacramental religion down the ages. A little more was conceded to the spirit of Catholic Modernism than Gore could ever have allowed.

A leading part in the shepherding of the intellectual effort of the newer Liberal Catholicism was taken by E. G. Selwyn (Rector of Redhill, Havant, 1919–1931, Dean of Winchester,

1931–1958). In his Editorship of *Theology* from 1920 he gave this school a platform. Theologically the reaction from Gore's position is best described in some words of Selwyn in his *An Approach to Christianity* (1925).

> These two schools may be distinguished for convenience as the historical and the analytical. The historical school, of which Dr. Gore is the foremost living exponent, takes its stand upon that element of simple testimony which is the original nucleus of the Gospel, and which consists for the most part of historical propositions; and it proceeds both to verify these facts by the recognized methods of historical inquiry and to draw out their doctrinal significance. The analytical school, on the other hand, works in to history rather than out from it. It regards the credal statements as in the first instance as symbols of spiritual experience; and its first concern is with those *credenda* which lie closest to this experience, irrespective of whether they contain a historical element or not. Furthermore, it insists very strongly that the Creeds should not be isolated from the rest of the thought process of which they form part, as though they were *sui generis*. Symbols of equal significance and truth may be found in liturgical forms, for instance, or in beliefs which never receive formal definition. On this view, doctrines like those of Grace or of the Real Presence rank *pari passu* with those of the Virgin Birth or the Resurrection of the Body (p. 245).

It is not hard to trace here a line of thought which had appeared nine years earlier in Sir Will Spens' *Belief and Practice*.

This was but one element in the movement of Liberal Catholicism in the period between the wars. Its greatest monument is *Essays Catholic and Critical* (1926) written under Selwyn's Editorship. This book was written in conscious succession to *Lux Mundi*, to which the authors in their Preface 'owe pre-eminent acknowledgment . . . a book which has exercised upon many of them a formative influence and still has a living message'. But in the intervening years there has come both a keener discernment of the *supernatural* element in religion, and a continuance of the *critical* movement with unabated vigour. The belief that the Catholic and the Critical elements are necessary to one another inspired the writing of the book. But whereas

Traditional Doctrines

Lux Mundi was in large measure a work of systematic theology, *Essays* was rather a work of apologetics.

The essays present less of a single coherent thesis than did *Lux Mundi*, and their significance lies in their illustration of a method and temper and in the great individual value of certain of their number. A. E. Taylor's apologetic essay, 'The Vindication of Religion', would alone bring distinction to any volume which contained it.

Some of the essays expound traditional doctrines with an eye upon the critical questions which have come to beset their presentation in the modern world. Thus L. S. Thornton on 'The Doctrine of God' considers specially the Creator's relation to the created world, and shews how the doctrine of the Trinity illuminates the problems. E. J. Bicknell on 'Sin and Original Sin' gathers up the discussions of many years upon the compatibility of evolution with the fall of mankind. J. K. Mozley on 'The Incarnation' shews the place of miracle and the doctrine of the two-natures as integral with the distinction between incarnation and immanence. K. E. Kirk on 'The Atonement' shews how the true corrective to an inadequate conception on purely exemplarist lines is a doctrine of Reparation by the Cross. In each of these essays orthodoxy is expounded with sensitivity to some particular problem of current doubt or denial. The reader feels the succession of *Lux Mundi*, not least in the moving essay by E. Milner-White on 'The Spirit and the Church in History'.

Other essays, however, plunge the reader more deeply into the contemporary critical world. E. C. Hoskyns on 'The Christ of the Synoptic Gospels', as we shall consider more fully in a subsequent lecture, uses the techniques of synoptic source criticism to shew the inadequacy of the Liberal Protestant reconstruction, and to draw out the unity between Christ and the apostolic Church. E. G. Selwyn on 'The Resurrection', while shewing powerfully the place of the event in the New Testament faith, interprets the appearances of the risen Christ by analogies drawn from the phenomena of Christian mysticism—a path along which few have since followed. N. P. Williams on

Liberal Catholicism

'The Origins of the Sacraments' dealt with a burning critical question: if the texts concerning direct dominical institution of the Sacraments are rejected on critical grounds, can we be sure that the Sacraments had origin in the intention of Christ and not in a borrowing from the mystery-religions? Williams' argument that the eschatological prediction in Mark 14: 24 found fulfilment in the Eucharist in the Church was felt by many to be more ingenious than convincing.[1] On the other hand, Will Spens on 'The Eucharist' drew out effectively two themes which he had specially made his own: the understanding of the Real Presence in terms of a 'complex of opportunities of experience', and of the Eucharistic Sacrifice in terms of the rôle of the Last Supper, and the Eucharist, in investing the event of Calvary with sacrificial meaning.

Catholic, critical, Biblical as they are, the essays did not present a coherent thesis in the manner of *Lux Mundi*, nor did they shew the thoroughly Biblical approach which was on its way to revival in English theology, though Hoskyns' essay was a harbinger of it. The book now seems somewhat dated, being later than the dogmatic theology of Gore and earlier than the return to the Biblical 'theology of crisis'. It now seems curious that the volume contained no theological treatment of the Old Testament, having instead an essay on 'The Emergence of Religion', and by-passes the issues of the Reformation in an essay (by Hamilton Thompson) which treats it mainly in political terms. Yet, despite these defects, the book still holds its own by the high distinction of some of its contents, and by being a genuine illustration of the quest at once of supernatural religion and critical integrity. It did immense service by shewing the possibility of that quest to many who were not attracted by Protestantism and yet had found Gore's position too rigid.

It is, however, in the essays on 'Authority' that we can best see where the newer Liberal Catholicism was contrasted with

---

[1] Dr. Ynge Brilioth made this shrewd and humorous comment, 'The eschatological conception is a dangerous handmaid, and may not be willing to leave on so short a notice as may be convenient for a Catholic employer.' *Theology*, November 1926, p. 282.

Acts of Belief

both the Tractarian and the *Lux Mundi* positions. Here is A. E. J. Rawlinson. The older idea of authority was, he says, that of pronouncements to be accepted, whether they be given by Bible or Church or Pope. This idea of authority must now be jettisoned. It does not hold its own, for it is palpable that those who accept authority in this way do so because its pronouncements correspond to something within their own experience, or because they make a series of acts of private judgment. Thinking out the doctrine of authority afresh, we can start from Tyrrell's conception of the authority of the experience of the 'millions', shewing that a set of religious practices and positions are vindicated if they (*a*) shew survival value, (*b*) mediate spiritual life of an intrinsically valuable kind. But this definition, says Rawlinson, does not suffice. Tyrrell's method can only shew that positions examined in this way can claim to embody *some* element of truth. How are we to justify the exclusive claim of a particular religious tradition when several may be rival claimants? There must, therefore, be a test, for Christian doctrine, of congruity with Scripture, and of congruity with reason.

> It should be the aim of the Church so to teach her doctrines as by her very manner of teaching to bear witness that they will stand ultimately the test of free inquiry and discussion, to teach them, in other words, not simply as the bare assertions of an essentially unverifiable authority, but as the expression of truths which are capable of being verified—spiritually verified in the experience of all her members; verified intellectually, as well as spiritually, in the reason and experience of her theologians and men of learning.

The weight of authority has degrees: what is genuinely 'ecumenical' is weightier than what is merely local.

At this point W. L. Knox takes over the discussion. He brings it home in a more practical way. What ought an individual Christian at any moment to believe? There are two distinct kinds of act of belief. (1) There is the act of faith in Jesus Christ, assisted no doubt by the testimony of the Church to Him, and ready to accept teaching of the Church as corollaries of the faith in Jesus Christ. (2) There is the act of faith in the Church, which accepts all that it says at the given moment because it is the Church which says it. The Roman Catholic Church upholds the second kind of belief—accept the Church, and believe everything that it tells you. The Anglican way is the former: belief in Christ comes first, and from that belief follows the accepting of teachings of the Church, authoritative because of their congruity with faith in Christ and because of their being rooted in the experience derived from that belief.

This treatment of authority left somewhat vague the nature and the limits of the Catholic Church as the organ of authority. Gore had held Catholicity to belong to a definable institution, with its authority tested by Scripture and by the moral fruits of its members. The younger writers appealed rather to the total stream of Christian experience, within which 'Catholic' Christianity represented certain norms of sacramental life and the types of saintliness which went with them. This shift of emphasis inevitably raised questions concerning the boundaries of the Church, and the significance of the religious experience of the Protestant Churches. These questions were promptly posed by a reviewer of the *Essays* in the *Expository Times*, and Selwyn answered them in the preface to a third edition. The question and the answer are of great significance. 'If', asks the reviewer, 'authority rests on Christian experience, surely those great Churches (Free, Lutheran, etc.) have some authority to plead. But if the Christian experience of these bodies is to count in assessing the authority of any truth, what becomes of the Anglo-Catholic contention?' Selwyn answers thus: 'The reviewer's question betrays a misunderstanding of the Anglo-Catholic claim. That claim is not that Anglo-Catholicism gives a final and exclusive expression of the truth, but that it represents the best expression at present available, in thought, worship and life, of the principles necessary to an ultimate synthesis.'[1] These words disclose the difference of the younger Catholic school from the older.

[1] *Essays Catholic and Critical*, third edition, p. vii.

Doctrines

V

The writers of *Essays Catholic and Critical*, and others akin to them, had considerable influence in the years between the wars. Their work fitted the mood of those whose minds demanded a critical spirit and whose souls craved for supernatural religion without being worried at a lack of coherence of system and authority. This school could reach out eirenically towards the Liberal Evangelicals and fulfil in many ways a mediating rôle. Its influence was very marked in the Report of the Archbishops' Commission on Doctrine in the Church of England. In several ways the writings of William Temple were akin to it, and so was the work of O. C. Quick, who—in detachment from any group or party in the Church—expounded a liberal orthodoxy, notably in his *Doctrines of the Creed* (1937). The ground was being cut from beneath the feet of Modernism.

The essayists themselves wrote much besides. Of the writings of Hoskyns a later chapter will speak. Rawlinson contributed notably to the vindication on critical lines of the unity of the New Testament presentation of the divine Christ, in his *Commentary on S. Mark* (1925) and in his Bampton Lectures on *The New Testament Doctrine of the Christ* (1926). N. P. Williams adorned historical theology in the massive learning and rotund rhetoric of his *Doctrines of the Fall and Original Sin* (1927). L. S. Thornton wrote one of the most notable works of the half-century, *The Incarnate Lord* (1928). K. E. Kirk had been breaking new ground in works on moral theology, and finding himself led on from moral theology to ascetical he wrote a great study of Christian spirituality through many phases of the West, *The Vision of God* (1931). In retrospect it is apparent that Kirk was detached from much of the prevailing liberal spirit of the time. While he had a competence in New Testament criticism akin to his contemporaries, he was in reaction from the pragmatism and the immanentism which he sensed as faults of the period. In lectures on *The Crisis of Christian Rationalism* (1936) he criticized Hegelian influences which still lingered in Anglican theology; and later in a Gore Memorial Lecture

Liberal Catholicism

entitled 'The Coherence of Christian Doctrine' he pleaded for that unity of dogma which the later Liberal Catholicism tended to obscure.

Was the transition from Gore to the younger school wholly one of gain? There was gain in critical freedom and in the possession of a less exclusively historical method. There was loss, as Kirk protested, in the grasp of dogmatic wholeness, and in the depth of moral intensity which was all Gore's own. Perhaps one work stands out as blending the excellencies of the two phases. I refer to A. E. Taylor's Gifford Lectures, published in 1930, with the name *The Faith of a Moralist*. Grappling with the nature of revelation, the place of the historical within it and the consequential concept of authority, Taylor seems to do justice to what the younger Anglo-Catholic theologians were seeking, while securing the essence of that for which Gore had stood so uncompromisingly.

Taylor's first volume follows the argument from conscience as it leads towards belief in God, in eternal life and in grace. The inclusion of the last of these is a distinctive part of the thesis and one which had not usually found a place within the 'moral argument'. The essence of the moral struggle concerns not only the will to pursue an ideal, but the will to be conformed to the ideal by a power upon which one depends. The bringing of 'grace' into the heart of the 'moral argument' gives the thesis both philosophic originality and religious depth. The second volume is concerned largely with the question: what is the place of the historical in revelation? It was Gore's question, and Taylor seems to fill some of the lacunae in Gore's treatment. Why is the historical event necessary to revelation? It depends on what revelation is about. If it is about the bringing of information from God to man, then it would not matter how the divine messages came—whether through many messengers or through some instructions other than the coming of messengers. But if revelation is about an actual interpenetration of the temporal by the eternal, the natural by the supernatural, 'bringing God down into the heart of temporality', then indeed

Process of Revelation

it will be the person and life in which the complete interpenetration of the eternal and the temporal has been actualized, which is itself the revelation, and to believe will be primarily not to assent to the utterances of a messenger, but to recognize the person, in whom the interpenetration of the two worlds has been achieved, for what he is. In a religion which still leaves God and Man, the eternal and the temporal, in their relative aloofness, the intermediary between them will be honoured for the message which he brings; but when the aloofness has been abolished in the unity of a person, then the sayings and the precepts of the intermediary will be honoured because they are his (Vol. II, pp. 122–123).

Such is Revelation, and its relation to history. What of Authority? Religion cannot be religion without the element of refractoriness to complete intellectual analysis, without refusing to supplement the statement 'this is what I can make of this situation' by the perilous addition, 'and this is all there is in it'. In natural knowledge, as well as in religion, there is a like 'humility before what is given to us'. A religion of revelation, if it is to remain such, calls for the docile receiving of what is given to us, together with intellectual adventurousness in the attempt to use it and to understand. There are always two factors in revelation: the contact with the supreme source, and the mediation of it by a contact with something or someone in time and history. Both these factors, the supernatural one and the natural one, are given by God.

I would not quarrel with anyone who felt that in this work of A. E. Taylor there is the finest flowering of the Liberal Catholic spirit. He shews how supernatural revelation evokes both childlike humility and adoration and the freest mental vigour in its assimilation in the thought of an age. He shews, with greater success than Gore, the synthesis of faith and criticism for which Gore had always striven. He does so because, while contrasting, like Gore, the supernatural and the natural, he is more able to shew the place of the latter within the single God-given process of revelation.

Liberal Catholicism found its days numbered with the coming of the Second World War. The movements towards dogma, and scholasticism, towards the transcendental theology of the

Liberal Catholicism

Word in the Bible, and away from the spirit of synthesis with the contemporary age, came in full flood. The categories of experience and piety, of evolution and apologetics, gave place to the categories of theology in its classic forms. The gulf seemed great: the denigrations across it were plentiful. But the questions asked by Liberal Catholicism have a way of returning, and are not to be pushed aside. Both the earlier and the later phases of Liberal Catholicism had their faults. If the faults of the later phase ought not to blind us to the importance of its quest, the faults of the earlier ought not to blind us to its perception of the coherence of the Christian faith.

CHAPTER EIGHT

THE HOLY CATHOLIC CHURCH

I

THE revival by the Tractarians of the doctrine of One Holy, Catholic and Apostolic Church went hand in hand with an immense emphasis upon the apostolical succession. They believed that it was in virtue of possessing a ministry with a commission handed down from the apostles that the Church of England was a part of the true Church. To the writers of the *Tracts for the Times* the significance of the doctrine was both ecclesiastical, as shewing that the Church of England was part of the Church Catholic and not merely an organ of national religion, and also moral, as demanding holiness on the part of those who held such a commission. It was an exclusive claim: 'We must', wrote Newman in the first of the *Tracts*, 'necessarily consider none to be *really* ordained who has not *thus* been ordained.'

With romantic enthusiasm, the Tractarians propagated this doctrine. In doing so they involved themselves in some misunderstandings of history and in some confusion of theology. As to history, they ascribed to the earlier Anglican divines an adherence to their own doctrine far more exclusive than was the fact, and they blurred the distinction between succession in office (which had been the particular theme of S. Irenaeus) and succession in consecration (which had become prominent in the teaching of S. Augustine). As to theology, they spoke of apostolical succession as the channel of the grace of the Holy Spirit in the Church in such wise as to do less than justice to His gracious activity within all the dispensations of the New Covenant. Hence arose a tendency to make apostolic succession itself the criterion of the presence of the visible Church in any part of the world.

The Holy Catholic Church

The Holy Catholic Church is, however, its own interpreter, and as the doctrine revived in the Church of England there came a greater discrimination in its understanding. The more Biblical and properly theological exposition of the doctrine of the Church by F. D. Maurice in *The Kingdom of Christ*, being somewhat apart from the controversies and leading conceptions of the time, exerted influence but slowly. It was the *Lux Mundi* school, and specially Charles Gore, who revised the Tractarian teaching in the light of a more discriminating appeal to Scripture and antiquity. Gore looked for broad foundations. The essential rôle of apostolic succession was in his mind bound up with other questions: the nature of Christianity as the religion of an institutional church, the rôle of all the members within that society, and the means of their unity with Christ and with one another.

The word 'Catholicism' meant for Gore 'that way of regarding Christianity which would see in it not merely or primarily a doctrine of salvation to be apprehended by individuals, but the establishment of a visible society as the one divinely constituted home of the great salvation, held together not only by the inward spirit but also by certain manifest and external institutions'.[1] This aspect of Christianity is congruous with the Incarnation, and rooted in the mission of Christ. Christ reconstituted the Church of Israel by a new covenant as a universal society. Into it people are received by Baptism, with the laying-on-of-hands in Confirmation as its completion and complement, and within it they are nourished in the Eucharist with the Body and Blood of Christ in union with His eternal sacrifice. Christ is prophet, priest and king, and His Church is a body through and through prophetic, priestly and kingly. If it was R. C. Moberly who specially drew out the priesthood of the whole Body as the context of ministerial priesthood,[2] Gore identified himself vigorously with the movement to enhance the place of the laity in the government of the Church.[3] His doctrine was far removed from

---

[1] *Catholicism and Roman Catholicism* (1923), p. 1.
[2] R. C. Moberly, *Ministerial Priesthood*, 1897.
[3] See *Essays in Church Reform*, edited by Charles Gore, 1898.

The Apostolate

clericalism. Yet the apostles and their successors rule and teach in Christ's name: 'the apostolic ministry in communion with which all the members of the body must remain'. 'To be a member of the Church meant from the first to be in communion with its officers, and in submission to their proper authority.'[1]

Gore traces within the Gospels the institution of the apostolate by Christ, and shews from the Acts and the Epistles how the apostles exercised in the Church an authority derived from Him. He claims that the evidence shews that the monarchial episcopate existing in the Church from the second century embodied the functions of the apostles, ruling, teaching, ordaining and serving as the bond of unity. The principle is that their authority is derived not from 'below', but from 'above'; it is bestowed by Christ through consecration at the hands of those with the authority to bestow it. It is the apostolic ministers who administer the sacraments; and the fact that the unworthiness of the minister does not render the grace of the sacraments inefficacious is congruous with that God-givenness of the Church's life which makes it in no wise dependent upon the character of its ministers, while it demands of them faithfulness, and judges them if they are unfaithful.

The Church with its institutional forms is thus the covenanted agent and home of salvation. Through its ministrations the Kingdom of God is present, and through it men enter the Kingdom of God. But Gore never allows the Church to be identified with the Kingdom. The Kingdom transcends it, and it ever prays 'Thy kingdom come'. The Church on its human side can bring upon itself scathing divine judgments, for worldliness, for arrogance, for moral distortion, for neglect of the living Word of God in the Scriptures.

Such is the true 'Catholicism'. The Church of Rome has distorted it, by claiming to be the whole when she is only a part, by substituting an authority which crushes the intellect for an authority parental and moral like that of Christ and the apostles, and by adding arbitrarily to the dogmas necessary for salvation. The Eastern Orthodox Church has retained the

[1] *Catholicism and Roman Catholicism*, p. 14.

essence of the true 'Catholicism' in continuity with the ancient and undivided Church, but without effective intellectual contact with the modern world. The Anglican Churches are wonderfully called to exhibit the true 'Catholicism' and to vindicate it by an adherence to its institutions together with a spirit of intellectual freedom and of moral fidelity to the Scriptures. Thus Gore described the Anglican vocation. He grieved, often and bitterly, that the Anglican response to it was hampered by worldly compromise with social injustice, by the moral weakness of its members and by lack of corporate principle in adhering to its own standards. He desired to see in England the Church disestablished and more conscious of its mission over against the materialism of contemporary civilization. Revival could not happen without first an awareness of the judgments of God.[1]

What of the Christian Communions which stemmed from the Reformation and lacked the apostolical succession? Gore was certain that, in repudiating the conception that authority to minister is given in the Church only by devolution from above, 'the Reformation Churches were—with whatever excuse—repudiating a law of divine authority in the Church, and also an essential principle of the Church's continuous life.'[2] True, they were vindicating certain divine principles: the supremacy of Scripture against the corruption of tradition, and the needs of liberty against spiritual tyranny: but, in their doing so, they were led to rebellious action which, in its turn, violated the truth about the nature of the Church. Gore would acknowledge—and those who knew him must needs realize how deeply he meant it —that the Holy Spirit had blessed and used the Protestant bodies in their witness; but, when pressed to adapt his ecclesiastical theory to that fact, he would answer that so also has the Holy Spirit blessed those who have repudiated the Sacraments, like the Quakers and the Salvationists. He also went on to say that, despite this divine blessing, the Churches founded purely

---

[1] Gore's doctrine of the Church is found in *The Church and the Ministry*, his fullest work, new edition revised by C. H. Turner, 1918; *Roman Catholic Claims*, 1893; and *Orders and Unity*, a popular discussion, 1908.

[2] *Orders and Unity*, p. 184.

Undenominational Religion

on Reformation principles had proved more and more fissiparous. Sects multiplied. 'The principles which justified the first secessions continue to justify new ones. Every fresh vision of the truth real or imaginary, but at least onesided, justifies a fresh organization. In this way English and American Protestantism present a deplorable picture.'[1] This picture Gore believed to be inherent in Protestantism realizing itself in history.

Furthermore, Gore noted the decline of the classical Reformation theologies. 'What force in Europe to-day is dogmatic Lutheranism, or the definite religion of Calvinism? How rapidly the distinctiveness of Baptist or Congregationalist or Methodist is merging in the common undenominational type of religion!'[2] Gore saw also in the decline of the fundamentalist idea of the Bible as the infallible Word of God a death-blow to what had been Protestantism's source of strength. He was, of course, reckoning with the liberalized Protestantism which seemed to dominate the field in the first two decades of the century. He did not foresee the revival of the classical Protestant systems, and the emergence within them of a new concern for the doctrine of the visible Church. Not foreseeing these events, he was confident that, with fidelity to her vocation, the Anglican Communion might gather to her own principles those who yearned for unity and could not accept it in the Roman Catholic form, and those who cherished intellectual liberty and would find it present only in the Anglican portion of the Catholic Church. In the principles underlying the Anglican Communion he saw a microcosm of Catholic unity, scriptural and liberal.

Besides dwelling much upon the Church in its scriptural descriptions as the Israel of God and the Body of Christ, Gore delighted to sum up the meaning of the Church in the phrase 'the extension of the Incarnation', a phrase which Jeremy Taylor had used of the Eucharist.[3] 'The Spirit', says Gore, 'is the life-giver, but the life with which He works in the Church is the life of the Incarnate, the life of Jesus.'[4] Very characteristic

---

[1] *Catholicism and Roman Catholicism*, p. 29.   [2] Ibid., p. 191.
[3] Jeremy Taylor, *The Worthy Communicant*, Chap. I, § 2.
[4] *The Incarnation of the Son of God*, p. 218.

The Holy Catholic Church

of Gore, this conception has come to be criticized as if it belittled the importance of the Cross or the Ascension for the Church.[1] Be it, however, remembered that for Gore the Christ whose Incarnation is completed in His saving presence in the Church through the ages is Christ in the fullness of His being as Crucified, Risen, Ascended and the Giver of the Spirit. It is this Christ whose presence and action in the Sacraments serve His indwelling in all the Church's members.

II

The conception of the Church, the apostolic succession and the Anglican vocation held by Charles Gore had immense influence. It deeply affected, though it did not wholly determine, the Anglican approach towards Christian reunion. But it had, in the course of time, to face the tests of criticism in relation to the history of the Early Church, the history of Anglicanism and empirical considerations drawn from the state of contemporary Christendom.

As to the Early Church, many Anglican scholars held that Gore's picture was too rigidly drawn. There had already been in the field the rather different presentation of the matter by Bishop Lightfoot in his famous *Dissertation on the Christian Ministry*. Lightfoot took a view different from what was to be Gore's about the transition in history between the primitive apostolate and the later monarchial episcopate. Lightfoot held that the episcopate was formed originally by the elevation of certain presbyters into a presiding position. Gore held that the process was by apostolic men like Timothy and Titus settling in particular localities. It is, however, possible to exaggerate the significance of this difference of view, since both scholars held the development to have happened by apostolic ordering, and Lightfoot drew this conclusion:

> If the preceding investigation be substantially correct, the three-fold ministry can be traced to apostolic direction; and short of an

---

[1] Cf. P. T. Forsyth, *The Church and the Sacraments*, pp. 81–84. L. Newbigin, *The Reunion of the Church*, pp. 59–62.

express statement we can possess no better assurance of a Divine appointment or at least a Divine sanction. If the facts do not allow us to unchurch other Christian communities differently organized, they may at least justify our jealous adhesion to a polity derived from this source (*S. Paul's Epistle to the Philippians*, 6th edition, p. 267).

Lightfoot is here typically Anglican in his cautious statement of the historical facts, and in his restraint in deriving principles from them. Looking to his cautious scholarship rather than to Gore's closely-knit conclusions, many Anglicans have rested content with some such account of the matter as this. Christ gave a distinctive commission to the twelve: the twelve, and certain others, are seen to exercise authority in His name: the subsequent episcopate which became the norm throughout the Church exercised functions of teaching, ruling, ordaining and shepherding the people of Christ, which the apostles had exercised, and were believed by the Church to possess a commission of authority bestowed on them through the apostles. The gaps in our knowledge, it is argued, do not affect the certainties which remain. If there is a 'tunnel' in the sub-apostolic period of which we have no knowledge, we know the ministry which entered the tunnel and the ministry which came out of it. If there is a 'development' it is analogous to that by which the Canon of Scripture and the Creed emerged from the apostolic teaching. If there is a divine gift determining the character of the Church in history, it is hard to separate Canon, Creed and Episcopate as being all part and parcel of that divine gift.

Not only the origin and the authority of the episcopate, but the meaning of 'succession' was much discussed within this period of Anglican theology. A. C. Headlam, in his Bampton Lectures for 1920 on *The Doctrine of the Church and Reunion*, dwelt much upon the contrast between the idea of succession held in the second century by S. Irenaeus and the idea of it held by S. Augustine and in the Church after his time. To the former, succession meant that Bishop followed bishop each in his see, and this continuity was an assurance of the handing down of sound doctrine. To the latter, succession implied more especially the link from consecrator to consecrated whereby the grace of order was handed on. It was this conception which came to have in some circles in the Western Church an unfortunately exclusive prominence as what has been called the 'pipe-line theory'. Yet consecration mattered in the earlier period, as it was in virtue of the authority given by consecration that each bishop performed his apostolic functions. No more discriminating account of these various distinctions may be found than in the important essay by C. H. Turner on 'Apostolic Succession' in *Essays on the Early History of the Church and the Ministry*, edited by H. B. Swete (1917). Turner also deals with superb lucidity with the difference between the Cyprianic conception of the validity of orders depending upon the authorization of the Church and the Augustinian conception of the life of the Church depending upon validity of orders—to give an all too simple description of an issue which has emerged in a modern form in discussions about unity.

It was one thing, however, to find in the primitive Church the norm of the Church's structure as catholic and apostolic. It was another thing to use that norm to decide the standing of Christian bodies within a divided Christendom. Here Gore found a large body of Anglican opinion at variance with him. The appeal to Anglican history shewed that a line of reputable Anglican divines held that the adherence of the Church of England to the apostolic orders as defined in the Preface to the Ordinal did not imply a denial of the orders of non-episcopal Reformed Churches, however much it implied the belief that the former orders were necessary for the 'perfection' of the Church. Gore was unshaken by such a consideration, for he was one of those who have looked for authority, not in an appeal to Anglican history so much as in the Anglican appeal to antiquity,[1] whose answer seemed to him decisive. Using the

---

[1] For a valuable exposition of the doctrine of the Church so treated, see H. B. Swete, *The Holy Catholic Church*, 1915. The appeal to antiquity in relation to the whole range of theology was uncompromisingly followed by Darwell Stone in various works: *Outlines of Christian Dogmas*, 1900, *The Christian Church*, 1905, and papers reprinted in F. L. Cross, *Darwell Stone*.

appeal to Scripture interpreted by antiquity, he saw in the primitive complex of Canon, Creed and Episcopate the norms of the One, Holy, Catholic and Apostolic Church as once given to the world; a divine human institution, now sadly divided, yet still able to witness to its God-given, divine–human character, a very part of a faith not to be modified by temporary phenomena like the post-Reformation societies (for such he believed them to be).

These societies, however, existed. They preached the Gospel. They were blessed by the Holy Spirit. What if the appeal to the ancient norms did not wholly interpret the position, and what if the ancient principle *ubi Christus, ibi ecclesia*, called for new assessments of ecclesiology? That became the crucial question.

III

A possible answer was that all Christian societies with an ordered ministry of Word and Sacrament were equally churches, and nothing more was needed than their mutual recognition and intercommunion. Anglicanism as a whole rejected that answer, through an instinct that whatever may or may not be necessary for the existence of a church, the historic episcopate was necessary for unity. Sometimes this instinct was expressed in terms pragmatic rather than theological. But there emerged a theological treatment of the issues which combined an empirical recognition of the spiritual facts of divided Christendom with an appeal to Scripture and antiquity for the norms of the One, Holy, Catholic Church of Christ. In the emergence of this theological treatment Archbishop Temple came to take a prominent part—here as elsewhere a disciple of Gore, yet with significant differences from him as well as continuity with him.

The famous Lambeth Quadrilateral, whose origin in the United States as the Chicago Quadrilateral of 1886 is an honoured event in the history of the American Church, began as a deliberate theological appeal to 'the principles of unity exemplified by the undivided Catholic Church during the first ages of its existence', and went on to name the Scriptures, the

The Holy Catholic Church

Nicene Creed, the two Sacraments and the Historic Episcopate as 'inherent parts of the sacred deposit'. The Lambeth Conference of 1888 endorsed the Chicago Quadrilateral, describing its items, however, not as 'inherent parts of the sacred deposit', but as 'a basis on which approach may be, by God's blessing, made towards Home Reunion'. It is well to recall the whole description.

(a) The Holy Scriptures of the Old and New Testaments as 'containing all things necessary to salvation', and as being the rule and ultimate standard of faith.
(b) The Apostles' Creed, as the Baptismal symbol; and the Nicene Creed, as the sufficient statement of the Christian faith.
(c) The two sacraments ordained by Christ Himself—Baptism and the Supper of the Lord—ministered with unfailing use of Christ's words of institution, and of the elements ordained by Him.
(d) The Historic Episcopate, locally adapted in the methods of its administration to the varying needs of the nations and peoples called of God into the unity of His Church.

That was the form of the Quadrilateral which came to be known during the next thirty-five years. The Lambeth Conference of 1920 in its 'Appeal to all Christian People' adhered to the same facts and principles; but it presented them in as conciliatory a way as possible, describing the fourth item as 'A ministry acknowledged by every part of the Church as possessing not only the inward call of the spirit, but also the commission of Christ and the authority of the whole body', and adding the question 'May we not reasonably claim that the episcopate is the one means of providing such a ministry?'

This conciliatory presentation aroused a great readiness to discuss reunion, and indeed inaugurated a new concern for it in many parts of Christendom. It went hand in hand with the most novel feature of the 1920 'Appeal', the avowal of the 'reality' of the ministries of the non-episcopal parts of Christendom. 'It is not', wrote the Lambeth Fathers, 'that we call in question for a moment the spiritual reality of those Communions which do not possess the episcopate. On the contrary, we

Free Church Ministries

thankfully acknowledge that those ministries have been manifestly blessed and owned by God as effective means of grace.'

The avowal about the non-episcopal ministries soon, however, created as many problems as it at first seemed to solve. A more explicit declaration was made by the writers of a Memorandum on the 'Status of the Existing Free Church Ministries' presented to the Joint Conference at Lambeth Palace on 6 July 1923. They describe them as 'real ministries of God's word and sacraments in the Universal Church'. But the next paragraph introduces the qualifying words, 'yet ministries, even when so regarded, may be in varying degrees irregular or defective'. The qualification produced feelings of frustration among the Free Churchmen, and went far to offset their enthusiastic reception of the original declaration. It had indeed been ambiguous. 'Spiritual reality' is a very ambiguous term; indeed, there were those, including an eminent member of the Lambeth Conference of 1920 and an ardent advocate of unity, who felt that ambiguity was present from the first.[1] There was no doubt as to the general Anglican mind in its unwillingness to un-church non-episcopal Christendom. But there remained a task of theological clarification and synthesis still to be done. At the Lambeth Conference of 1930 the Report on the Unity of the Church, produced under the Chairmanship of Archbishop Temple of York, gave a lucid theological exposition of the rôle of the episcopate in the Church, its authority as a development parallel to the Canon of Scripture and the Creed, and its embodiment of 'the original conception of the apostolic ministry'. Whereas Lambeth 1920 had presented episcopacy in a pragmatic way, Lambeth 1930 gave what may fairly be called a classic theological exposition.

It is not my purpose, however, to trace events: but to record the movement of theological thought which formed their background. The need was for a theology *de ecclesia* which did justice both to the wide dispersion of God's spiritual gifts in a divided Christendom and to the place of the episcopate as the God-given bond of unity and continuity.

[1] Cf. H. H. Henson, *Retrospect of an Unimportant Life*, Vol. II, p. 20.

There were those content to say that all the ordered Christian communities adhering to the Scriptures and the two dominical sacraments were equally 'Churches', so long as they had ministries appointed by laying-on of hands with prayer, and that the status of their ministries need not be questioned—being all equally 'valid', if the term 'valid' be used. Episcopacy was, however, necessary or desirable to achieve unity. A. C. Headlam's Bampton Lectures were the most considerable expression of this view. There were, however, those who, unable to accept Headlam's view on account of their more theological understanding of episcopacy, none the less felt the need for some qualification of their catholic doctrine in virtue of contemporary facts. These had a hard theological task, and I would refer to some of their attempts to meet it.

A landmark is seen in the volume of Bishop Paddock Lectures by T. A. Lacey on *Unity and Schism* (1917). Lacey was a High Churchman and a scholar of considerable powers. His theme was that the whole Catholic Church was 'in schism', torn in separately organized pieces, maimed on its human side in every part, yet possessing the unity of 'race' in the underlying brotherhood of all the baptised—a unity which endured despite the divisions on other levels. 'Sirs, ye are brethren.' The identification of denominations with churches was utterly wrong: the need was not to unite the denominations, but to bring deliverance from them into that catholicity of faith, life and institution which expressed outwardly the underlying brotherhood. This deliverance could not come by papalism or by federalism, or by intercommunion, or by episcopacy as such, but by an integral catholicity described in terms a little reminiscent of F. D. Maurice. Lacey's theme had a theological and spiritual depth which was easily missed by those who subsequently drew upon it. His repudiation of the identification of Church and denomination is too often forgotten. But few missed his cardinal point that schism is *within* the Church.

It was no doubt Lacey's influence which was seen to some extent in N. P. Williams' essay on 'The Theology of the Catholic Movement' in *Northern Catholicism* (1933). Williams dis-

Validity of Orders

tinguished the Catholic Church in the stricter sense as identifiable with an inner circle of Christendom—itself divided—which possessed the full catholic and apostolic institutions, while around it was the outer circle of Christian communities which lacked in various degrees the marks of catholicity.

There was, however, a particular theory drawn by O. C. Quick from the idea of internal and universal schism. It was the theory that in a divided Christendom all orders and sacraments are not equally valid, but have their validity impaired. You will find this theory worked out by Quick, both in his volume on *The Christian Sacraments* and in his *Doctrines of the Creed*. Believing that the apostolic succession was the ministry proper to the Church's being as an organism linked with the Incarnation, Quick identified validity not with the possession of certain powers, but with the possession of authority to act, within the Church, in the name of Christ and of the whole Church. We should return not to the Augustinian view that the Church depends upon the existence of a ministry with indelible powers, but to the Cyprianic view that valid orders are those which possess the authority of the whole Church. 'Validity of orders depends upon the unity of the whole body within which holy orders are conferred and exercised.' This leads to the radical conclusion: 'Once admit that part of the essence of orders is an authority conferred in such a manner as to implicate the whole body of the Church as one, and in a divided Church the validity of orders becomes inevitably a matter of degree.' All are in schism. All orders are relatively invalid. 'Perhaps God has concluded all under the sin of schism that He may in the end have mercy on all through the grace of union.'

Quick's theory supplied what seemed to be new moral possibilities, for all can acknowledge their own defects. The urgent need is the extension everywhere of the one Church order which, until it is extended everywhere, lacks the full authority of Christ in His Church. If we speak of what others lack, we find our own lack to be grievous, till all are one. Quick's theory had great influence, and various reunion schemes have subconsciously reflected it. But with the passage of time it has been found to be

The Holy Catholic Church

vulnerable, in that it gives insufficient weight to the transmission of authority in the Church and to the fact that the 'whole Church' in whose name a man ministers is not just the sum total of contemporary Christians, but a body reaching across the generations. It was on this issue that William Temple was to provide a corrective. To his teaching about the Church and the ministry we now turn.

IV

It is beyond the scope of this book to describe Temple's immense work for Christian unity as one of the architects of the oecumenical movement from the Faith and Order Conferences of Lausanne and Edinburgh to the initiation of the World Council of Churches. Our concern is with the theology of the Church which inspired him. His biographer notices the movement of his mind in a catholic direction, as he grew in the realization of the integral place of the Church in the Gospel and of the apostolic succession in the Church. Yet with this he combined a deep conviction of the principle *ubi Christus, ibi ecclesia,* which expressed itself in his wholehearted acceptance of the various Lambeth Conference utterances on the reality of non-episcopal ministries.

How did Temple synthesize the two elements in his thought? I should like to quote a private letter dated 29 April 1936, which I received from him when I was a very young theologian.

> Can you at all accept an analogy which appeals to me? I utterly believe that the four strands—Scripture, Creeds, Sacraments, episcopal ministry—are essential strands in the union of the Christian or Branch with the Body of Christ or True Vine. But if a Branch is partly severed, it still lives with the life of the tree. It suffers from the lack of the form of connection that is lost; it lives by what is left, and it is still a part of the tree. . . . I could only agree to union or to any approach to full intercommunion on the basis of the agreement that all future ordinations are episcopal. But, if that is agreed, I would go far in recognizing the *de facto* efficacy of the existing ministries. And I greatly respect the con-

The Historic Ministry

cern of Free Churchmen lest in accepting (re)ordination they should in fact strengthen the hold of the vicious theory which has grown out of Augustine's handling of the Donatists.

Temple did not endorse Quick's theory that all Orders are relatively invalid as a result of Christendom being divided. Rather did he hold that the historic ministry remained what it was in the fullness of authority in spite of the separation of portions of Christendom from it. Like Quick, Temple dwelt upon the possession of authority rather than the possession of powers; but he held that authority to minister in the name of the whole Church was not derived from contemporary Christendom, but was handed down by the appropriate organs of the Church. Here are words in which Temple put this with great lucidity. After quoting the statement that certain ministries are real ministries and yet 'in varying degrees irregular or defective', he writes:

> In other words, though real ministries within the universal Church, they may still not be ministries *of* the universal Church with a commission from the whole fellowship to all its members. Our claim is that where a living Church acts through duly consecrated Bishops we have assurance that there Christ bestows His commission, which is a commission to act on behalf of the universal Church. If some part of the Church refuses to recognize it, that will constitute a defect in the effectiveness of the commission, but it will not destroy it as a commission of the Universal Church. For it is Christ who gives the commission through the Church, His Body.[1]

Here we see clearly where Temple's difference from Quick's theory lies. The divisions in Christendom did not prevent the historic ministry from being still the ministry *of* the One, Catholic and Apostolic Church of Christ in distinction from ministries which are *not that*.

Another passage brings out still further the depth of Temple's thought, and the delicate balance of its presentation:

> When I consecrate a godly and well-learned man to the office and work of a Bishop in the Church of God, I do not act as a representative of the Church, if by that is meant the whole number of

[1] *Thoughts on Some Problems of the Day*, p. 114.

contemporary Christians; but I do act as the ministerial instrument of Christ in His Body, the Church. The authority by which I act is His, transmitted to me through His apostles and those to whom they committed it; I hold it neither from the Church nor apart from the Church, but from Christ in the Church. . . . This authority to consecrate and ordain is itself witness to the continuity of the life of the Church in its unceasing dependence on its Head, Jesus Christ, who is the same yesterday, today and for ever. Every priest who by virtue of his ordination celebrates the Holy Communion acts not for the congregation there present, nor for all Christian people then living on the earth, but as the organ of the Body of Christ, the ministerial instrument of Christ active in and through His Body; so that though no more than two or three persons be actually assembled, yet the congregation at that Holy Communion is the Communion of Saints, with which the persons present, be they few or many, are there conjoined. Here, therefore, as in the Incarnation itself, we find the eternal in the midst of time, the secret of a fellowship against which the gates of death cannot prevail (Convocation of Canterbury, 25 May 1943. *The Church Looks Forward*, p. 24).

The context of these words is important. Temple was speaking of the proposed United Church of South India, pleading that there, as elsewhere, Anglicans should not 'make difficult the access of others' to 'the Apostolic Ministry', and that during the necessary period of transition anomalies should be accepted, including the existence within the United Church of ministries which, though 'irregular', had been 'owned and blessed by God'. Temple would dwell, not upon what various Christian communities lacked or possessed, but upon what they would come, through union, to share together. This would be, not some new Church created by the fusion of the denominations, but the One, Holy, Catholic Church already existing and handed down the ages with the 'apostolic ministry' as (already) the effectual sign of its continuity and its given-ness. Temple's words reflect a depth of thought about the nature of the Church as a divine–human organism reaching across the centuries, and a rare balance of expression about the relation therein of Church and ministry. It is doubtful whether such words could have been written in 1920, for they reflect the deeper grasp of the

Faith and Order

theology of the Church which had come in the intervening years.

Between 1920 and 1943 theological change had been considerable, and in no respect more than in a new realization of the doctrine of the Church.[1] Temple himself wrote in 1939: 'Theologians of to-day are more concerned than we were in 1910 or 1920 with the theological status of the Church.... Hence there is a new appreciation of the importance of the Church for faith itself... we did not fail a quarter of a century ago to insist on the necessity and claim of the Church. But this was secondary; now it is basic and primary.'[2] Whereas in 1920 it was possible for the Lambeth Fathers to treat 'unity' as an isolated concept without drawing out its theological content and relation to the other attributes of the Church, the words of William Temple to his Convocation in 1943 which I have quoted relate 'unity' to the other dimensions of the Church's being and refuse to treat 'unity' solely in terms of the Church's contemporary manifestation.

In the understanding of the Church it seems a considerable step from Gore to Temple. To an extent which Gore would never allow, Temple allowed the facts of a divided Christendom to modify his presentation of the doctrine. He affirmed the positive significance of the non-episcopal communions; and while order had for him deep theological meaning, he could never say, as Gore said boldly, that faith and order were equated in divine revelation.[3] Devoted to the procedure of analysis and synthesis, Temple was convinced that beneath every strongly held position there is some truth to be extricated and cherished. All things to all men in the understanding of people and of ideas, he had a rare sympathy with every

[1] Cf. E. Mersch, *Le Corps Mystique du Christ*, 1923; H. de Lubac, *Catholicisme*, 1937, G. Gloege, *Reichgottes und Kirche im Neuen Testament*, 1929; K. L. Schmidt, art. 'ecclesia' in *Wörterbuch zum Neuen Testament*, 1938; C. H. Dodd, *History and the Gospel*, 1937; A. M. Ramsey, *The Gospel and the Catholic Church*, 1936; L. S. Thornton, *The Common Life in the Body of Christ*, 1943.

[2] W. Temple, 'Theology Today', *Theology*, November 1939.

[3] Gore, *The Church and the Ministry*, p. 73.

The Holy Catholic Church

half-light, as well as with what he believed to be the clear light of catholic truth; and he abhorred the drawing of negative corollaries from positive principles or from uncertain ones. With unselfconscious charity, he was one with any and every group of believers in Christ in the realization of what he shared with them.

It was this difference of Temple from Gore which enabled him to do his work of reconciliation in the service of Christian unity. Yet the convictions which he shared with Gore stand out no less in the perspective of Anglican history. In the appeal to Scripture and antiquity, Temple, no less than Gore, found as the God-given supernatural fact 'the wonderful and sacred mystery' of the One, Holy, Catholic and Apostolic Church of Christ.

CHAPTER NINE

THE RECOVERY OF THE BIBLE

I

THE title of this chapter is a paradox. It describes what is indubitably true, for none of us would question that, in a deep sense, the Bible has 'come back'. Yet were not the years which we have been studying years in which the Bible was always in the middle of the theological scene? A line of great scholars devoted themselves to it: Driver, Sanday, Streeter, Turner, Stanton, Burkitt, Lake. Teachers and prophets expounded it. The philosophical theologians had its revelation as the datum of their systems. The most urgent controversies were about the historical facts which it describes. And it never ceased for Anglicans to be the authority and rule of faith. With the Bible always in the midst, how may we speak of the return of the Bible?

The question is not hard to answer: but the answer is a little complex. It is found partly in the incarnational character of the dominant Anglican theology, partly in the cultural climate of the period, partly in the scope of the Biblical studies which were most prominent, partly in the methods and interests of theological education in a particular phase of its development.

We have seen already in the second lecture of this series that, when the Incarnation becomes the centre of theological system and exposition, the result may be a deep and rich orthodoxy standing firmly upon a Biblical basis, yet with a tendency for other Biblical themes to recede. There is no doubt that this happened in the first years of the twentieth century. Again, the art of presenting the orthodox faith in close relation to a civilization dominated by the ideas of moral and social progress can unwittingly cause the Christian teacher to blind his eye to the perspectives of grace, judgment, wrath, mercy which the Bible

The Recovery of the Bible

presents. The cultural environment of a theology can so seep into the tone of its presentation as hardly to leave its content unaffected. It is interesting to recall that most Anglican teachers at the time of the 1914-18 war did not (Charles Gore being a glowing exception) see it in terms of the Biblical idea of judgment, but rather as a bitter and sorrowful delay in the march of that progress which is indeed the Kingdom of God.

The period is indeed memorable for the work of New Testament scholarship. At Cambridge the successors of the great trio of the previous century continued the work of criticism and exegesis: Armitage Robinson, Swete, Stanton, Burkitt. At Oxford, Sanday, Turner, Streeter and others were of the same calibre. But what was the work? It was in the main the work of investigating the historical foundations—work of which the results were sometimes radical, sometimes conservative, but work of which the chief interest was to discover what elements of historical fact emerge from the critical study of the documents. The concentration was *there*, rather than upon the drawing out of the theology which the documents contain. It was in line with this concentration that a concern about the 'life of Jesus' (and a supremely necessary concern at all times), rather than a concern about the Gospel of God in Jesus, determined the scope and method of the study of the Gospels. A parallel state of things prevailed in Old Testament studies. Historical research saw the history and religion of the Jews as a part of the general movement of history and religion in the ancient East: when so seen, the uniqueness of the religion of the Jews becomes palpable, and the first steps are made towards a theological assessment of their Scriptures. But in this period it was the historical stage which was uppermost in study and teaching. The unity of the two covenants and the theological significance of the whole were not much in evidence. While H. F. Hamilton's *The People of God* (1912) was a forewarning of a different kind of interest, it is significant that even in 1926 *Essays Catholic and Critical* dealt with 'The Emergence of Religion' and not with the theology of the Old Testament.

Now in the realm of educational method these tendencies

Need for Critical Theology

were even more apparent. It had not been so very long ago that the old fundamentalist ideas were still in vogue in church and school. The pedagogic need was for long years felt to be to vindicate critical methods and to teach people to use them. Hence, right down to the 1914–18 war, and indeed after, 'theology' in the ancient English universities largely meant the analytical work of literary criticism in relation to the historical reconstruction of Christian origins. As assumptions are inevitably made by any student, the assumptions in this case could easily be those of very partial scientific principles. Inevitably also, a wedge was driven for many students between this partial science on the one hand and their thinking about God, Christian truth, religion on the other. In such a state of things Biblical study will not lead to theological understanding of the Bible; and Christian doctrine, while appealing to the Bible, will not be interwoven as it should be with the most scientific Biblical exegesis.

Such were the causes of a sort of unhappiness which often beset the student of theology in the second decade of the century, and indeed beyond. It meant that the great doctrinal teaching which existed in the Church was not related enough to the Biblical scholarship of the time. It meant that those who replied to Modernism in the name of orthodoxy did not sufficiently stand on their adversaries' own critical ground with the same scientific weapons. It meant that those who studied the Bible had too many impediments to grasping why it is, what it is and what it really says. Certainly the remedy could not come in any retreat from the rigour of critical method. The need was for a more profoundly critical theology in which both noun and adjective had their fullest meaning.

II

To many Anglicans, as indeed to many who were not, it was Edwyn Clement Hoskyns who became the symbol of what seemed a startlingly new approach to the Bible. Hoskyns, as a young man, had not achieved academic success. An undergraduate at Jesus College, Cambridge, he read history, and was known as one with wide human sympathies and a firm Anglican loyalty, drawn from his father, who became Bishop of Southwell. It was in a time spent in Berlin, after taking his degree in 1907, that Hoskyns was stirred to both a passion for theology and a care for scientific, scholarly method. His powers developed late. 'Harnack taught one to try and think things out for oneself, Cambridge never taught me that.' This naughty sentence comes from a paper entitled *Die Oxford Bewegung* given by Hoskyns in Germany in his early years in the Anglican ministry.[1] In this paper he paid enthusiastic tribute to the scientific spirit of German Biblical study; but added, 'But he who would gain a sense for the Church, he rather remains in England. Personally, I am convinced that in the Oxford Movement there is the key to the understanding of the Church.' Another quotation from an early unpublished paper of Hoskyns hints at what was to be most characteristic of him as a teacher: 'It is a tremendous truth that religion spells mystery, and that mystery cannot be put into so many words. Oh, the accursed theologians of the past, who seem to have been present at the making of the world, or instead of being on their knees with the Cross are sitting on the throne of God asking him questions. When once theology loses its humility, consign it to the refuse-bin' (from MSS.).

It was after some ten years—a curacy in Sunderland, the wardenship of a hostel in Sheffield University, a chaplaincy in the first world war—that Hoskyns found his supreme opportunity as Fellow and Lecturer in Divinity at Corpus Christi College, Cambridge, from 1919.

Hoskyns' lectures on the Theology and Ethics of the New Testament were an exciting experience for us who heard them in the nineteen-twenties. They were exciting because of the clash between them and the assumptions upon which academic theology normally proceeded at the time: the assumption that there had been a primitive simple Gospel of Jesus which had been progressively elaborated and obscured by the apostolic

[1] Quoted by J. O. Cobham: 'Hoskyns, the Sunderland Curate' in *Church Quarterly Review*, July–September 1957.

Moral and Social Progress

theology, and the assumption that it was unscientific to bring to the study of the documents any considerations of a religious kind—such as an appreciation of the nature of Christian religious experience. With these assumptions Hoskyns made a head-on collision. He would begin with the religious experience of the Church in the apostolic age, telling us frankly that our own religious experience was not irrelevant to our understanding of the documents. We were given a fascinating discussion of New Testament Greek, shewing how the religious experience had affected the character of the language. From the apostolic theology, moulded as it was by the Church's experience of the risen Lord, Hoskyns went back to the history which lay behind it. Here he made rigorous use of the discipline of synoptic criticism—a discipline in which he required exacting standards in his pupils.[1] Criticizing the prevailing critics, he shewed that in every stratum of the literary sources the sayings of Jesus imply a messianic mission and a breaking-in of the reign of God through His words, works and death. Clearly, theological study had something to do with religion, and with the life of the Church.

In retrospect, I doubt whether the novelty and provocation of Hoskyns' lectures were due entirely to the contrast with the more familiar theological procedures of the time. Rather was the clash between the discovery of the New Testament which Hoskyns was making for us and the general ethos of religious culture in which his hearers shared, whether liberal or orthodox, Nonconformist or Anglican. It was the deeply-rooted assumption that Christianity was bound up with moral and social progress, that the Kingdom of God was the steady enlargement of all that is good in the world. What was strange and foreign was the idea that the Kingdom of God meant the breaking-in of the divine righteousness in a particular history in such wise that moral idealism was itself under judgment. The knife was being put not only into conscious theological tenets, but also into the half-conscious assumptions of our common ethical culture.

[1] I was not directly Hoskyns' pupil, being of another college.

The Recovery of the Bible

Hoskyns wrote within a few years these significant works: an essay on 'The Christ of the Synoptic Gospels' in *Essays Catholic and Critical* (1926); an essay on 'Jesus, the Messiah' in *Mysterium Christi* (1930); and the volume *The Riddle of the New Testament* in collaboration with Noel Davey (1931). I think that the first of these is the most brilliant and cogent.

The essay is perhaps the most effective answer to the Liberal Protestant thesis, accepting and using to the full the same tools of scientific method which the liberals had used, and fairly claiming to use them more scientifically. It is in the particular field of the criticism of the Gospels that Hoskyns there engages. He lays down certain scientific principles which he says are too frequently ignored in reconstructions of the story of Christian origins. (1) Passages which are found only in later sources should not be dismissed as necessarily originating at the date of the source in which they are found. (2) Editorial corrections of an older document are not necessarily bad corrections. (3) If a word occurs only in a late document it does not follow that what is expressed by the word is secondary (e.g., the word *ecclesia*, which comes in the Gospels only twice in Matthew). (4) Where there are in a document distinct strata of subject matter it must not be presumed that the dates of their origin can be arranged in a definite chronological order. (5) Where a word in an ancient document can be paraphrased by a word in use at a later period it does not follow that the original is best reproduced by such a paraphrase. Urging that the neglect of these criteria had vitiated the Liberal Protestant thesis, Hoskyns makes his own examination of the literary strata, and finds in all of them the same main themes: the messianic kingdom, the presence of the kingdom in the words and works of Jesus, the divine necessity of His death, His future coming in glory, the disciples sharing in His humiliation, the disciples sharing in His glory.

The conclusion is strikingly put.

> A whole series of contrasts underlie the synoptic tradition. These contrasts, however, do not break the unity of the whole, since they are capable of synthesis. The failure of most modern scholars to

formulate the contrasts correctly has led to their failure to recognize the possibility of a synthesis. The contrast is *not* between the Jesus of history and the Christ of faith, *but* between the Christ humiliated and the Christ returning in glory . . . *not* between a reformed and an unreformed Judaism, *but* between Judaism and the new supernatural order by which it is at once destroyed and fulfilled . . . *not* between the disciples of a Jewish prophet and the members of an ecclesiastically ordered sacramental cultus, *but* between the disciples of Jesus who are as yet ignorant of His claims and of the significance of their own conversion, and the same disciples, initiated into the mystery of His Person and of His life and death, leading the mission to the world, the patriarchs of the new Israel of God. . . . Thus stated the contrasts are capable of synthesis by a fairly simple view of history. Judaism is fulfilled by the advent of the Christ, who inaugurates the new order which is the Kingdom of God on earth. The existence, however, of the Kingdom of God and of the kingdoms of this world together involves conflict and opposition which is to last till the return of the Christ and the final destruction of evil, when the Kingdom of God will come on earth as it is in heaven.

What follows?

The historian is freed from the necessity of being compelled to assume that a foreign influence was exerted upon primitive Christianity between the crucifixion and the appearance of the earliest Pauline Epistles, and he is therefore enabled to treat the development represented by the Pauline Epistles, the Johannine writings, and the literature of the Catholic Church primarily as a spontaneous Christian development.

In retrospect, the *lacuna* in Hoskyns' thesis is that in his treatment of the critical question he neglects the pre-literary stage of Gospel-tradition on which Form-Criticism was already placing much emphasis. But in his exclusive concentration upon literary source-criticism he was on common ground with those in this country with whom he was arguing. It was in keeping with our insularity that Form-Criticism, in vogue in Germany since 1918, hardly made itself felt in England until the nineteen-thirties. These facts, while they diminish the permanent value of Hoskyns' work, do not lessen its achievement as a scientific victory amid the conditions of their time.

The thesis of this essay was elaborated in *The Riddle of the*

New Testament in relation not to the Gospels alone, but to the apostolic writings generally. These writings are inexplicable except as created and controlled by a particular history, itself inexplicable except as the redeeming act of God in the mission, death and resurrection of Jesus. This book led very many of the clergy and the laity to read the Gospels with new eyes. Eyes were opened to the Old Testament background, everywhere present, as Jesus fulfils and transforms the mission determined for Him by the Scriptures: and eyes were opened no less to the loneliness and majesty of Jesus in S. Mark—the other evangelists 'nowhere heighten Mark's tremendous conception'. This Jesus is a scandal to humanitarianism. To those who were shocked by this claim Hoskyns had his answer: 'The primitive Christians found the revelation of God in an historical figure so desperately human that there emerged within the Early Church a faith in men and women so deeply rooted as to make modern humanitarianism seem doctrinaire and trivial.'

At first, it appeared that Hoskyns' influence was on the side of Anglo-Catholic churchmanship. So indeed it was, for Hoskyns was vindicating the unity between Jesus and the Church with its supernatural, sacramental life. Hoskyns had contributed a forceful pamphlet, *Christ and Catholicism*, to the 'Congress Books' series in 1923, and at the Anglo-Catholic Congress of 1927 he delivered a paper on 'The Eucharist in the New Testament', in which he defended Catholic eucharistic belief against the attacks which were being made upon it at the time by Bishop Barnes of Birmingham, and concluded with the words, 'Our controversy with the Bishop of Birmingham and those whom he represents does not concern primarily the Eucharist but the Gospel. In this particular controversy it must in any case be stated, and stated clearly, that we Catholics have the New Testament wholly on our side' (*Report of the Anglo-Catholic Congress*, 1927, p. 56). Hoskyns also spoke at the Congress of 1930, with the 'Apostolicity of the Church' as his subject. Some words may be quoted as significant of the trend of his thought. He still speaks of the continuity of the Church with the Gospel, but he dwells also on the subjection of the Church

Recovery of the Bible

to the Gospel. 'Taught by the New Testament, we are bound to think of the Episcopate as preserving the witness of the apostles and to demand this of the Bishops. The Bishops are not mystical persons to whom we owe some strange kind of undefined mysterious obedience. The Bishops are responsible to bear witness to Jesus Christ, the Son of God, and to hold the Church to that witness' (*Report of the Anglo-Catholic Congress*, 1930, p. 88). Such is the supremacy of the divine word by which the Church is judged.

While it is therefore true that Hoskyns for some years provided 'grist for the Anglo-Catholic mill', it was increasingly seen that his significance was not exactly that. It was the recovery of the Bible that was the issue: the Bible as the theologians' absorbing concern, the Bible in those sharp, scandalous, challenging notes which had been soft-pedalled for several generations. Very soon those whom Hoskyns had excited realized that he was but a part of an excitement stirring many parts of Christendom.

It became customary to describe Hoskyns as a Barthian. We must ask how exceedingly limited is the sense in which that is true. It is doubtful whether Hoskyns was acquainted with Barth's writings before the nineteen-thirties, when he translated Barth's *Römerbrief*. He was never the disciple of the teacher, still less of the system. He was not interested in the Dogmatic Theology to which Barth was turning. What I think Hoskyns chiefly got from Barth, through his work of translation—itself a literary achievement—was *eloquence, language*. He caught something of Barth's tone of speech and mode of expression: incisive, passionate, paradoxical. Perhaps, also, he got from Barth a deepening of his own perception that the Biblical theologian exists not to be commending a system, but to be constantly subjecting every attempt at system to be judged by the Cross. Nothing became more characteristic of Hoskyns than the distinction he constantly made between 'theology' and 'propaganda'. To indulge in the latter was to betray the theologian's task.

These aspects of Hoskyns' theology are apparent in his published sermons.[1] The sermons were all delivered in the Chapel

[1] *Cambridge Sermons*, E. C. Hoskyns, 1940.

of Corpus Christi College in the years from 1926 to 1935. It goes without saying that they are uncompromisingly theological: but it is no less evident that they are written in a very down-to-earth way for a particular human situation. This is particularly so in the course on 'The Vocabulary of the New Testament, the Language of the Church'. The Church has a language: it possesses words and phrases—and the ones which figure in these sermons are, World, Neighbour, Now—Then, Here—There, Tribulation—Comfort, Flesh—Blood, Spirit, Weak—Strong. 'The Church does not require of us that we should master a new vocabulary, but that we should apprehend the meaning of the commonest words in our language; it demands that we should not, at the critical moment, turn away from the meaning of words, but that we should wrestle with them and refuse to let them go.' These Christian words describe things as they are; and it is the rôle of the Church not to manipulate things by propaganda, but to describe them as they are and to shew how they point to God. The sermon on 'The Neighbour' strikes at sentimental ideas of brotherhood and fellowship, and draws out the significance of the uncomfortable difference of our neighbour from us:

> Sentimentalize our neighbour, and we shall sentimentalize God. Clip off from our neighbour all that he is which differs from us, and we shall assuredly trim God to our own measure. Regard our neighbour as the reflection of ourselves, instead of one who enters disturbingly into the world we make for ourselves, and we shall certainly make of God an idol like us, and we shall fall down and worship it. In that contradiction of nearness and remoteness which every neighbour is, we see the signpost which directs us towards the God who is other than we are.

A series of sermons on the Thirty-Nine Articles [1] shew Hoskyns recapturing the Augustinian strain in the Anglican tradition, a strain which had come to be often forgotten or apologized for. Seldom can the Articles have been approached in a more down-to-earth manner.

[1] *Church Quarterly Review*, July–September 1958.

Justification by Faith

God manifests Himself in the rough and tumble of human life, and our ultimate destiny emerges from this rough and tumble. Consequently, if you read the Thirty-Nine Articles, you are not reading a theological discourse spun out of the quiet, reflective training of men remote from the world. You are reading statements wrung out of controversy; more than that, wrung passionately out of the complete insecurity of life, and written in the blood of men.

It is the state of human insecurity which lies behind those Articles which 'continually make the avowal of human inadequacy'. 'Have we so little sympathy with our ancestors, or so little knowledge of the deep scepticism concerning men and women which reverberates through the literature of our day . . . to be unable to perceive the evident sincerity of these Articles?' It is from that background that Hoskyns drew out the meaning of Justification by Faith.

Hoskyns died in 1937, after a short and sudden illness, not yet 55. Three years after his death there was published, through Noel Davey's editorial care, his commentary on the Fourth Gospel. It is a theological commentary, devoted not only to expounding the theology of John, but to shewing how that theology springs from the witness of the apostolic Church to Christ, and is related to the theology of the New Testament as a whole. The clue to Hoskyns' approach appears in the fascinating section of his Introduction, in which he traces the history of the interpretation of the Fourth Gospel in modern scholarship. On the one side were interpreters who, parting company with any idea that the book is substantially historical, had found its significance as a non-historical work which reinterprets the Christian faith in terms of Hellenism or mysticism (Holtzmann, Loisy, E. F. Scott, Inge). On the other side, English scholars in the main had defended the historical elements in the Fourth Gospel and protested against the extravagances of the extreme critics; but, by making it their business to save what portions they could for historicity and to do no more, they were failing to find the secret of the book or to explain its character as a whole (Lightfoot, Sanday, Stanton, Bernard). Scott Holland, in Hoskyns' view, had excelled all the more recent writers on the Fourth Gospel by approaching it with theological insight and by recovering the theological interest of Westcott. Holland's greatness lay in the fact that he did not treat the Fourth Gospel as a problem: rather did he find that the Synoptists were a problem, in that they left so much unexplained, and that John gives the clue to their meaning and unlocks their secrets.

Hoskyns argued that the Fourth Gospel was written against the false spiritualizing or mysticizing of Christianity which the first Johannine Epistle describes. The evangelist says, 'Back to history'. The Word was made flesh. It is in the flesh of the Son of God that salvation comes. There is no passing beyond it: no substitution or 'spirituality' for it, or adding 'spirituality' to it. But the history is not to be studied, proved or enjoyed as something intelligible in itself, for it is intelligible only when it points beyond itself to God. 'The flesh profiteth nothing': yet 'Except ye eat the flesh of the Son of Man and drink his blood, ye have no life in you.'

It has been a serious criticism of Hoskyns that he virtually ignored the Hellenistic background of the Fourth Gospel. He concentrated on the relation of the book to rabbinic teaching, to the Old Testament and to the rest of the New Testament, excelling in the way he shews how themes scattered and implicit in the first three Gospels became explicit in the Fourth. It is a no less serious criticism that, the problem of authorship receiving little examination, questions about historicity are somewhat evaded. Allowing that history means fact plus meaning, and that the Fourth Gospel is concerned with meaning, it is none the less inevitable to ask, more pressingly than Hoskyns ever asked, what happened and what does the evangelist himself believe to have happened. It is here that we see a weakness which has been more and more apparent as Biblical theology has advanced.

III

'The reading of it has been an illuminating and exciting experience. Hoskyns has made the Fourth Gospel speak with a

Validity of the Bible

clear voice to our generation.' Such was the tribute of C. H. Dodd. The word 'exciting' is significant. Hoskyns, and Dodd himself, were among those who in the nineteen-thirties excited many to the Bible, its unity, its urgency, the validity of its own categories.

In this connection, how should the influence of Karl Barth within Anglican circles be assessed? Never influential among us in his dogmatic theology, he had no little influence as a prophetic teacher. He was in a sense a sort of experience through which many Anglicans passed.

It seems that the first Anglican who studied Karl Barth carefully was C. J. Shebbeare, the learned Rector of Stanhope in County Durham—where Butler had been Rector two centuries before. In a remarkable essay in a now-forgotten composite volume, *The Atonement in History and Life* (1930), Shebbeare gives an account of Barth's teaching drawn from the original German of the Commentary upon Romans. Here we see an Anglican's first reactions. He finds in Barth an overwhelming sense of the gulf between God and man—alike in his good works and in his piety. 'To wish to conceive such a world as this as one with God, is either religious arrogance, or the ultimate insight which comes from God.' 'To get the ultimate insight we must withdraw the penultimate insight from circulation.' 'Only the captive becomes free, only the poor becomes rich; only the Nothing becomes Something.' Shebbeare saw in Barth a revival of familiar themes of Protestant theology—the worthlessness of works or piety as a means of justifying men before God. But he found in Barth also a new dimension both of anti-Pelagianism and of anti-Rationalism, and in comparison with it the Reformation theology itself seemed tame. Here was Existential theology, and the idea of Dialectic Revelation. Theology is *existential* in that man is not free to admire or to judge of its content: like Nicodemus, he finds himself judged by it, his own existence challenged, the ground cut from under his feet. Revelation is *dialectic* inasmuch as any straight proposition about God must mislead us in the very act of our receiving it—since any words we use are inadequate and our thoughts are not God's

The Recovery of the Bible

thoughts. It is therefore only in paradox that God's word comes through to us. 'The righteousness of God is the "nevertheless" by which He associates us with Himself and declares Himself to be our God. Thus "nevertheless" contradicts every human "consequently", and is itself incomprehensible and without cause or occasion, because it is the "nevertheless" of God.'

As the teaching of Karl Barth began to be known in the English-speaking world,[1] sometimes neat and sometimes through the somewhat diluting medium of Emil Brunner, what was the effect on Anglicans? Very few indeed were led to an interest in Barth's dogmatic theology: rather more were led to an interest in classical Reformation theology. But there were many more who, without being drawn from one theological system to another, underwent a theological and religious 'shock'. It was the 'shock' of facing, with a starkness we had not seen before, the contrasts: God—Man, Creator—Creature, God—the World. It was the 'shock' of realizing that our knowledge and grasp of divine truth can be totally perverted through becoming a thing of 'ours', a possession to enjoy and defend, so that ultimately it witnesses to ourselves and not to God. The difference came home between faith on the one hand, and piety and religion on the other.[2] To some who were Anglicans the influence of Barth affected their attitude to the Bible and the Church. In their reading of the Bible the themes of the living God, election, judgment, the death of Christ as the 'stripping from himself of all human possibilities', the Resurrection as the advent of something 'beyond', the last things, came alive in a new way. In their attitude to the Church and the sacraments there was the purging of the idea that here is a system to be defended and commended as a thing in itself. Rather is the Church known by faith as the place where sinners are humbled under the Cross, and know thereby the glory of the Resurrection, witnessing,

[1] An English translation of *Das Wort Gottes und die Theologie* appeared in 1928.

[2] This distinction had been made in the teachings of Fr. H. H. Kelly, founder of the society of the Sacred Mission, Kelham, who used to dwell upon the contrast, learnt from F. D. Maurice, between theology and religion. See Kelly, *The Gospel of God*, 1928.

Interpretation of Scripture

obeying, but never propaganding, apologizing or self-commending. The doctrine remained the same, but it passed through a kind of dark night into a new day.

In the nineteen-thirties the recovery of the Bible was very consciously felt in many ways within the Church of England. There was the shift of interest from criticism to theological exposition. There was the new grasp of the Old Testament not as an episode in the development of religion, but as the story of God's redemptive acts from Moses to the Messiah. There was the new grasp of the unity of the Bible arising from the appreciation of the single theme of redemption and the redeemed people of God who runs through it. There was the new realization of the unity between the historical Jesus and the apostolic preaching and theology. There was the tendency to see the New Testament not as a patchwork of different interpretations, but as possessing in the apostolic preaching an inner core of unity: a theme which had considerable vogue through the influence of C. H. Dodd. The effects of Biblical study were passing powerfully to many of the parochial clergy and the teachers in the schools. The idea of the interpretation of Scripture by Scripture became prominent, and if Hoskyns' *Fourth Gospel* was one signal illustration of it, another was seen soon after in L. S. Thornton's *The Common Life in the Body of Christ* (1942), a massive work of New Testament interpretation, without the typological eccentricity subsequently to appear in Thornton's writings. Some words in the Preface are significant, where Thornton recalls that in *The Incarnate Lord* he had made an attempt 'to relate the revelation of God in Christ to current philosophy', and adds, 'What if the Gospel becomes obscured by our presuppositions and preoccupations, so that we neither see the scope of its application nor suffer it to speak for itself?'

Within this Biblical movement the doctrine of the Church had a big place. It came to be more and more perceived that the Gospel and the Church belong together, and are a part of one another. It followed that Evangelical Churchmen become more aware of the Church's place within the Gospel. It followed also that High Churchmen, while finding the importance of the

Church to be vindicated, tended to see it less as the extension of the Incarnation with the Bible to justify its origin, and more from within the Bible itself as the elect race and the body of Christ. The tendency was both enhanced theologically and brought within the practical life of the Church by the 'liturgical movement', for the first impact of this movement came to England from the Continent in this period, and was made widely known through Fr. Gabriel Hebert's influential book, *Liturgy and Society*. The liturgy was now seen less exclusively in the doctrinal categories of presence and sacrifice, and more comprehensively as the whole mystery of Christ recapitulated in the rite. Within the liturgy the divine action in consecration, sacrifice and communion was seen to be joined with the ministry of the divine word in Scripture and sermon. Together, Biblical and liturgical revival has brought a greater unity within the Church of England.

The rediscovery of the Church within the Bible, and the Bible within the Church, carried many Anglicans far away from the apologetic liberalism or apologetic catholicism of an earlier generation; and many became aware that a similar discovery was happening in other parts of Christendom, and that near at hand Nonconformist scholars were assisting and leading the process. A new *milieu* of converse was appearing for Anglicans with Free Churchmen in this country, and with Lutherans and Reformed in other countries, as a result of theological development within which Roman Catholics also had had their part. In the Oecumenical Movement which increased its momentum in the later nineteen-thirties these newly aroused conceptions of Bible and Church were very influential. But naïve ideas that unity was just round the corner had to face certain contrary facts: for there were also revivals of self-conscious confessionalism in the various Christian communions.

It is, therefore, no exaggeration to speak of the recovery of the Bible. Those who have as theologians known the second, third and fourth decades of this century have experienced the changes easier to feel than to describe. The changes have had causes very diverse: social disillusionment and international cata-

Biblical Theology

strophe, the teaching of certain prophetic figures, the scientific work of many scholars. If I have chosen to give space to Hoskyns it is not because I am unmindful of others among whom he is but one, but because in his own environment he was lonely and creative, and an arresting sign of the times. The story of Biblical theology has run on beyond the half-century which we are studying, and it runs on still. Its achievements have continued long enough to create in turn some formidable problems. It has been possible for theology so to concentrate upon the exposition of the Bible 'from within', that its relation to other categories of thought can be evaded. It has been possible so to conduct theological exposition of the Bible that questions of history are treated with less seriousness than is due to them. Both these tendencies invite reactions and revenges, creating the problems which theology now has to face.

CHAPTER TEN

WILLIAM TEMPLE

I

THE name of William Temple has already come many times into our story. We have seen something of his thought about the Incarnation, about miracle, about the Cross and about the Church. It is time that we looked at him and his theology with more concentrated gaze. He had dedicated one of his earlier books [1] to Gore, describing him as 'one from whom I have learnt more than any other now living of the spirit of Christianity, and to whom more than any other (despite great differences) I owe my degree of apprehension of its truth'. The contrast between the two is a big one. Gore was from the first a theologian by training and profession: grounded in the exact discipline of the Bible and the Fathers. Temple came to theology from philosophy by a journey through several stages; and in a sense his theology was that of an amateur.

The amateur can, however, have a keen eye for significance, and it was this that Temple brought to theology again and again. We have seen already how his interest in particular doctrines was for the sake of their bearing upon theology proper, upon God. Thus the kenotic question interested him less for what it suggests about the mode of the Incarnation than for what it suggests about divine omnipotence and love. Atonement interested him not only for the sake of us men and our salvation, but for what he believed it to tell us of sacrifice in the heart of the eternal Godhead. Miracle, at which he had at one time stumbled, came to matter to him for his belief that God is personal. The visible Church was significant as a sacrament of eternity in the midst of time. Thus, if Temple was the amateur,

[1] *Studies in the Spirit and Truth of Christianity*, 1917.

Experience of Human Life

he was yet, *par excellence*, the theologian. For him, *everything* was related to God, and to be cherished and studied in that relation. Both as a thinker and as a man Temple had a vast circumference of human interests and an unchanging centre, for all his interests were united serenely in his faith. Religious experience was for him the experience of anything and everything. He was thus, if ever a man was, theologian by temperament and intuition.

Temple's wide experience of human life—the philosophy don, the schoolmaster, the founder of the Workers' Educational Association, the London rector, the canon of Westminster, the bishop of industrial Manchester, the Archbishop of York—was a part of his approach to theology no less than to statesmanship. Intellectually, it was Temple's method to start from the circumference and work towards the centre. He did not begin with dogma, he led up to it as the answer. Characteristically, his first considerable book, *Mens Creatrix*, passes through metaphysics, art, tragedy, morals, politics, education, before it reaches theology as the unifying principle. Intellectually, Temple took some time before he could be sure of orthodoxy; but, religiously, it is probable that he had never doubted God or Christ. It has been remarked that, for all his many questionings, he was seldom troubled much by questions of New Testament criticism, and could even treat them rather naïvely, as in the introduction to his exposition of S. John. This is evidence of the 'believing propensity', which W. R. Matthews ascribed to him.[1] Here again is one of the contrasts between Gore and Temple: Gore, ever wearing the scars of doubt and conflict as to the love of God, but sure that the orthodox Creed with its miracles was the only one which made God and His love credible; Temple, serene in his faith in Christ, but searching long as to whether the orthodox understanding of that faith were the true one.

[1] *William Temple, An Estimate and an Appreciation*, p. 9.

II

Temple sought, first for himself and then for others whom he would help, to build bridges from the idealistic philosophy he had learnt from Caird and Bosanquet to the faith of the Incarnation. He felt that the philosophical climate of the time was friendly to a spiritual interpretation of the world, unfriendly to a particular revelation. It was credible that God and men could be united in the whole process of the world, scarcely credible that deity could do things in particular. Against such assumptions Temple set himself to vindicate, in idealism's own terms, the rationality of an Incarnation and a particular revelation. It has to be discussed whether in the midst of this process he retained modes of thought more Hegelian than were really compatible with a Christian view of God's relation to the world.

Mens Creatrix (1916) had built the bridge. *Christus Veritas* (1924) was a theological exposition of the result, Temple's first, and perhaps greatest, full-scale work in theology proper, written during his Manchester episcopate. He argues from the significance of mind to the supremacy of value, and from the emerging series Matter, Life, Mind, Spirit, to the Incarnation as the grade of reality in which humanity is fulfilled. The treatment of the Incarnation is marked by a particular emphasis upon the Two Wills, but without the uneasiness about the term 'substance' which had appeared in his essay in *Foundations*. The Incarnation is the unveiling of Godhead; and of its tremendous corollaries none is more significant than that God is Christ-like, and in Him is no unChrist-likeness at all. Thus the suffering love of the Incarnate is the key to the working of the divine omnipotence; and the dereliction on Calvary does not conflict with Christ's deity so much as shew the meaning of divine love. Temple's thought is intensely Johannine, the glory of Calvary being one with the glory which the Son had with the Father in the unity of the Spirit before the world began. In terms of love and glory we see the meaning of the Trinity, the nature of heaven as men's goal, the mode of the divine government of the processes of nature and history, the significance of suffering. It

The Hegelian Strain

is fair to say of *Christus Veritas* that no book on the Incarnation is more religious or more comprehensive in relating the world with the central fact of Christ which illuminates it. It illustrates a saying of Temple's that his whole theological thinking was the effort to see the full meaning of the words 'he that hath seen me hath seen the Father'.

The critical reader of *Christus Veritas* may, however, find himself puzzled not only by a strain which is very near to patripassianism,[1] but by a suggestion that the temporal experience of the Incarnate somehow added to the perfection of the divine love: and he may wonder whether too much concession is not being made to Hegelian assumptions. The crucial passage on this is on p. 280: 'God eternally is what we see in Christ; but temporally the Incarnation, the taking of Manhood into God, was a real *enrichment* of the Divine life.' We have to ask how far the Hegelian strain in Temple's thought persisted, both in *Christus Veritas* and in the Gifford Lectures on *Nature, Man and God* (1934), where Temple defends, at greater length, the rationality of a particular Incarnation.

The Hegelian strain seems to appear in Temple's treatment both of the relation of God to the world and of the problem of evil. (1) In the tradition of Biblical thought, the world of space and time is not necessary to God's existence or perfection: it depends upon Him utterly, owing all to Him as He owes nought to it, for it exists through the will of One who is infinite in His perfection. (2) Again, in the tradition of Biblical thought, evil is not to be understood as rationally explicable as the condition of the highest good, so that good and evil constitute a single and intelligible whole: it is a grim reality which must be changed in *fact* before the world can become intelligible for thought. It was there that Gore, for instance, was content to leave the matter: freedom was a certainty, its misuse was no part of a rational 'scheme of things'. Temple, however, gave more than a suggestion that the world is necessary to God's perfection as God, and that evil is a necessary element in the highest good and a part of the rational unity of things.

[1] Cf. pp. 58–59 of the present work.

William Temple

As to the first question, Temple contrasted what he called the 'naïve mythological view' of God's relation to the universe with the view which he held philosophy to require, and he sought to present a synthesis of the two. 'In the sense in which God is necessary to the world, the world is simply not necessary to God. Apart from Him, it has no being; apart from it, He is Himself in plenitude of being.' We should concur. But what, then, of this sentence? 'Even to the eternal life of God, His created universe is sacramental of Himself. If He had no creatures to redeem, or if He had not redeemed them, He would not be what He is.' It is hard to doubt that this latter statement shews a subordination of the Biblical and patristic view, and of the postulates of the Christian worship of God, to the needs of idealistic metaphysics. It seems to be akin to the view which sees in the Blessed Trinity the description of God's relation to the world and identifies the creation of the world with the begetting of the Son, rather than the view which worships the Blessed Trinity as the perfection of Majesty and Love upon which the world utterly depends.

As to the second question, Temple was, it seems, guided by two philosophical considerations. One was the desire to 'make sense' of freedom, sin and goodness as rationally coherent. The other was the desire to 'make sense' of the concept of divine love which reveals itself in its most characteristic glory in terms of sacrifice, which in turn involves the creative use of suffering in the conquest of sin. Both these quests of rationality lead Temple very near to making sin a part of the unity of the divinely ordered universe, so near indeed that he wrote: 'It is true to say that God so made the world that man was likely to sin, and the dawn of moral self-consciousness was likely to be more of a "fall" than of an "ascent". Human sin was not a necessary episode in the divine plan, but was always so closely implicated with the divine plan that it must be held to fall within the divine purpose.'

In both these ways Temple was saying what was hard to reconcile with some of the intuitions of orthodoxy: the sense of the total dependence of creation upon a Creator perfect in

Treatment of Revelation

Himself, the sense of sin as an unspeakable distortion of the divine plan, such as cannot be contemplated as capable of rationality or synthesis. Both these intuitions were ones which Temple himself knew and shared, for none understood more than he both the meaning of Adoration and the jealousy of the divine Righteousness. It was the philosophy with which he was working which caused him to write as he did in his search for synthesis; and it would not be difficult to answer him by quotations from himself. He did not live to modify these particular pieces of Hegelian influence on his thinking, so much as to affirm that the quests of theology must needs radically change their ground. The darkening skies made theologies of explanation and synthesis seem irrelevant, and caused theologies of redemption to replace them. We shall see before the end of this lecture how William Temple acknowledged this change: 'The world of today is one of which no Christian map can be made. . . . Our task with this world is not to explain it, but to convert it.'

There was, however, in Temple's theological construction an element whose influence has been more continuous, namely his treatment of Revelation. He refused to divide the works of God into those which constitute revelation and those which offer none. 'Unless all existence is a medium of revelation, no particular revelation is possible. . . . Either all occurrences are in some degree revelation of God, or else there is no such revelation at all. . . . Only if God is revealed in the rising of the sun in the sky can He be revealed in the rising of a son of man from the dead.'[1] This is because the God who reveals Himself even in the most exceptional occurrences is revealed as the Lord of *all* occurrences. Yet whereas God's action in events for the most part follows a pattern describable as 'the uniformity of nature', whenever He interrupts this uniformity it is 'an expression of the divine character in face of critical situations, and not only an episode in the age-long activity of God'.[2] Hence the term revelation may be used *specially* of these occurrences which happen in the history of men rather than in the ample spaces of nature. Furthermore, the fullness of this revelation can be given

[1] *Nature, Man and God*, p. 306.   [2] Ibid., p. 305.

only in a person, inasmuch as we who are persons can only fully understand what is personal; and God being personal cannot otherwise reveal Himself adequately.

How does this happen? Not through a set of propositions. There are no revealed propositions; and it is incorrect to speak of 'revealed truths', though it is right to speak of 'the truth of revelation'. It happens through events wrought by God and minds inspired to interpret them. It is in 'the intercourse of mind and event' that revelation happens: 'the coincidence of divinely controlled event and mind divinely illumined to read it aright'.[1] The event itself is the objective datum of revelation, the interpretation in its subjective concomitant. Revelation having happened in the event, the doctrines of the Church about it follow as its correct formulation. But the faith which receives the revelation is not primarily the holding of correct doctrines: it is the response of a man to what the living God gives him in the event, it is fellowship with the living God through Christ. The Christian does not believe in the Creeds so much as use the Creeds to describe, aid and formulate his belief in God through Christ. Christ the revelation of God is infallible; but we have no infallible knowledge of Him in the records or infallible statements in the Bible.

Temple's teaching about Revelation has had immense influence. It was congruous with much in the trend of English theology since *Lux Mundi*, and of liberal theology generally since Ritschl; and while it treated the event as primary, and faith as a relation to a Person, it conserved the importance of dogma in a way that Ritschlianism never did. But it is as a theory vulnerable. The distinction between history as objective and interpretation as subjective breaks down, since it is hard to define history except as event *plus* interpretation. The distinction between the stage of event and the stage of proposition breaks down, since interpretative propositions enter into the very record of the events. Nor, if the dogmas are necessary to enable the revelation to be conserved by the Church and grasped by the faithful, can they be held to lie outside the act of

---

[1] *Revelation, A Symposium*, p. 107.

Influence on the Church

revelation. These criticisms suggest that Temple's formulation of the nature of revelation considerably over-simplifies the issues with a measure of false antithesis.

None the less, Temple's thesis concerning revelation, vulnerable as it may be, has had a most salutary influence. It has helped in the recovery of the Biblical view that in revelation events come first, and that the idea of a corpus of revealed propositions standing on its own ground is intolerable. It has helped to keep central the conviction that it is towards a Person that faith is directed, and that revelation is dominated by that fact. Temple's presentation brings to the centre what should be at the centre, and thus helps us on our way towards a comprehensive view of revelation in which event and interpretation, Person, proposition and inspired imagery have each its own place.

III

Temple's writings were, however, but one factor in his immense influence upon the theological life of the Church. With his rare understanding of various movements in contemporary thought he won a rare measure of trust in himself, and, with his bent for synthesis, he did much to interpret different movements to one another. He was able to converse as a theologian with men of other mental disciplines, and he was able to teach theology to the people. Glimpses of that influence remain in the mind: Temple holding a church full of people during an August bank holiday at Blackpool with his expositions of the Apocalypse, Temple discoursing to the Aquinas Society on the philosophy of S. Thomas, Temple described in a letter of E. K. Talbot to Lord Halifax as 'the one bishop of the older generation to whom the younger theologians listen with respect and who carries authority with them'.[1] Temple never spoke to a wide circle with more effect than by his *Readings in the Gospel of S. John*. Let it suffice to quote the tribute of Reinhold Niebuhr: 'I think it

[1] The Earl of Halifax, *Fulness of Days*, p. 168.

represents a new medium in the combination of scholarly and devotional treatment.'

Of the creative part taken by Temple in the movement for Christian unity, I spoke in an earlier lecture. By infecting others with his conviction that some truth lurks behind every erroneous position, he did more than any other man to spread the habit whereby Christian traditions look at one another for self-criticism and learning rather than for the vindication of their own excellence. Yet into this process of mutual edification Temple brought his conviction of the Holy Catholic Church of Christ, whose visible order is a part of its essence as a sacrament of the Incarnation.

Of Temple's teaching on a Christian social order others have written with the fullness which the plan of this book precludes.[1] I say a few words only of the theology from which the teaching sprang. Whereas Gore had treated social problems partly in terms of a prophetic denunciation of evil, and partly in terms of the Church as the brotherhood following 'the way' in the midst of an unrighteous world, Temple, possessing as he did a doctrine of the State as well as of the Church, was more ready as a social thinker to trace the lines of a divine order of society, and as the ground for this he turned increasingly to the concept of Natural Law. He saw Natural Law as giving the key to the proper functions of State, family, property and trade, and he came to esteem highly the Thomist conception of the Just Price and the Prohibition of Usury. Believing in a divine order, he had a high conception of the Church's rôle to permeate society with the right conviction of its possibility, and this caused him to be far less antagonistic than Gore to the establishment of the Church. Unless and until the State desires to cast off its union with the Church, let the Church retain that union as a burden to be borne in the service of the community. Temple pressed for the degree of autonomy for the Church represented by the Enabling Act of 1919, which Gore regarded as an utterly inadequate measure of freedom. But Temple refused to press

[1] Cf. especially M. B. Reckitt, *Maurice to Temple*, the Scott Holland Lectures for 1946.

Theological Trends

for disestablishment after the rejection by Parliament of the Revised Prayer Book in 1927 and 1928, at the time when Hensley Henson came out vigorously for the radical policy. I ask you to notice the theory of the social order, for the sake of which Temple valued establishment.

It is, however, of Temple's influence upon theological trends within the Church of England that I would say rather more. In the nineteen-twenties there was much theological energy, and no little conflict. There was the conflict between tradition and Modernism, with the Girton Conference of 1921 as its focus. There was the conflict on eucharistic doctrine and practice which gathered impetus around the revision of the Prayer Book in 1927 and 1928. There was the constant conflict of tendencies about Christian reunion, some looking first to the English Free Churches, and others to the Eastern Orthodox or to Rome. In the next decade, however, cutting across these controversies, there were the newer movements, Karl Barth, 'Biblical Theology', the liturgical movement. Throughout these phases Temple had no small eirenic influence in helping to interpret movements, and generations, to one another.

Anglo-Catholicism reached a peak of fervour and confidence in the nineteen-twenties. In part influenced by the Liberal Catholic ideas of the generation younger than Gore, in part more conservative and traditional, in part receptive of the influences of Counter-Reformation spirituality and devotional practice, this movement grew.[1] As a *conscious* movement it had begun to recede before the end of the period, partly because some of its salient principles were now widely diffused in the Church and its counsels, and partly because the newer movements in Bible and Liturgy tended to engage the enthusiasm of younger people. Evangelicalism, meanwhile, underwent some considerable changes. The old guard of conservative evangelicalism remained. But a 'Liberal Evangelicalism' emerged, with

[1] Cf. W. L. Knox, *The Catholic Movement in the Church of England*, 1923, for the more 'extreme' presentation, blending both the Latin and the liberal; T. A. Lacey, *The Anglo-Catholic Faith*, 1926, for a view original and modern, yet more in the Tractarian stream.

William Temple

the stamp of the nineteen-twenties conspicuously upon it.[1] This was a broad-minded Evangelicalism, ready to be more sacramental, more scholarly and more eirenic. It did much for the spirit of synthesis in the Church, and it led in the cause of Home Reunion. But it was somewhat vulnerable to the superficial liberal, progressivist ideas of the time. As our period ends, it was beginning to give place to the newer 'theological' brand of Evangelicalism now in greater prominence.

The pressures of controversy in the nineteen-twenties caused a great desire to see how far theological understanding and synthesis might be found within the Church. In response to that desire Archbishop Davidson somewhat reluctantly agreed to the appointment in 1921 of the 'Commission on Doctrine in the Church of England', a body of twenty-five theologians charged 'to consider the nature and grounds of Christian doctrine with a view to demonstrating the extent of existing agreement within the Church of England, and with a view to investigating how it is possible to remove or diminish existing differences'. The Commission contained scholars of very diverse outlook; its work took fifteen years, and it was not until 1937 that its Report was issued. The original chairman had been Bishop Burge of Oxford; but he died after little more than two years, and William Temple took his place. It was not the rôle of the Commissioners to define the doctrine of the Church or to lay down what its limits ought to be. Rather was it the task to provide a *speculum* of what in fact was thought and believed by theologians within the Church of England, with such indications of synthesis as were possible.

The result was a volume of 240 pages of very varying value. The portions dealing with the doctrine of God, revelation, authority, Incarnation and Redemption faithfully indicated the diversities of belief, but failed to probe adequately into the background of assumptions which lie at the root of the diversities. This weakness is startling. The ability for the task was present among the Commission. But perhaps this failure goes to

[1] See the volume of Essays, *Liberal Evangelicalism*, 1922, and the writings of V. F. Storr.

Commission on Doctrine

shew that a discussion-group method cannot grapple with fundamental thinking in the way that individuals sometimes can. On the other hand, the portions dealing with Church, ministry and sacraments—particularly the last—are fuller, and provide what are really substantial essays of high value, still eminently worth the reading.

The question asked of any work of this kind is *Quo tendimus?* As regards orthodoxy, many readers noted that the Report recorded the presence of theologians who held that the empty tomb was not an essential part of the Resurrection faith; and the presence also of those who held that a natural birth rather than a miraculous one befits the Incarnation of the Son of God. More perspicacious readers, however, noticed that the Report shewed how great had been the recession from what had been some of the main postulates of Modernism in the nineteen-twenties. Thus, the view that sin is the anachronistic survival of animal traits, the view that God and man are of one nature in such wise that perfect humanity is to be identified with deity, the view that *only* the exemplarist or Abelardian doctrine of the Atonement has validity—these views now found no place at all within this comprehensive *speculum* of Anglican thought. The change is remarkable. Particular interpretations of doctrine on liberal Modernist lines remained: but the dogmatic assumptions of Modernism had mostly vanished from the scene. If any one standpoint is relatively conspicuous within the Report, it is perhaps the standpoint of the younger Liberal Catholicism. But the Report is too faithful a *speculum* for any sort of monopolies to be present.

The treatment of the Sacraments is thorough, with the most useful analysis of conceptions such as validity, sacrifice, presence. On sacrifice the summary conclusion is worth quoting:

> The Eucharist is a corporate act of the Church towards God, wherein it is united with its Lord, victorious and triumphant, Himself both priest and victim in the sacrifice of the Cross. This connection has been expressed in at least four ways: (1) through stress on the union of ourselves with Christ in the act of communion, and

in that union the offering of 'the sacrifice of praise and thanksgiving' and of 'ourselves, our souls and bodies'—a view generally held in the Church of England, many members of which would find here alone the sacrificial element in the rite; (2) through emphasis on the fact that in the Eucharist we repeat the words and acts of Christ at the last supper in words and acts whereby it is held that He invested His approaching death with the character of a sacrifice; (3) through the insistence that the rite is a representation before the Father of the actual sacrifice of the Cross; (4) through the doctrine of the Heavenly Altar, at which we join in the perpetual offering by Christ of Himself, and share the life of Christ crucified and risen.... There are those who would combine all the views stated, while some of them would be repudiated in certain quarters. We consider that all of them should be regarded as legitimate in the Church of England, and we are agreed in general terms in holding that the Eucharist may be rightly termed a sacrifice—which we have defined as 'an act in which man worships God, the form of the act being an expression of the homage due from the creature to the creator'. But if the Eucharist is thus spoken of as a sacrifice, it must be understood as a sacrifice in which (to speak as exactly as the subject allows) we do not offer Christ but where Christ unites us with Himself in the self-offering of the life that was 'obedient unto death, yea the death of the Cross'.

I quote these words as they are a good illustration of the way in which the Report provides a *speculum*, and assists a synthesis.

It is less easy to illustrate by quotation the section upon the Eucharistic Presence. Not only does it draw out the eucharistic beliefs traditional and legitimate within Anglicanism, 'the Real Presence' and 'the receptionist doctrine', but it shews the variety of modes in which modern thought has enabled the former doctrine to be expressed. Thus the Eucharistic Presence may be expressed in terms of 'value', or in terms of 'a complex of opportunities of experience', or in terms of the bread and wine being taken up into a new relation to the living Christ so as to be His Body and Blood 'simply through Christ's use of them to be the very means of His self-communication'. The discussion is eirenic inasmuch as it is made clear on the one hand that 'Receptionism' need not carry the subjective associations commonly attributed to it by its critics; and of the last of the modes of expres-

Transition

sion of the Real Presence described above it is said: 'Many of those who value the Receptionist strain in our doctrine can understand and feel at home with a doctrine of the Real Presence as thus stated.' There is also an analysis of the uses of the terms 'body and blood' in eucharistic thought: (1) The identity of the body of His flesh, now glorified, with the eucharistic body, (2) the eucharistic body as the organ of His presence akin to the use of 'Christ's body' to describe the Church, (3) the body and the blood as that of which the bread and wine are effectual signs. A little more dated than the pages on sacrifice, those which deal with the Eucharistic Presence are a monument of eirenic scholarship.

I have tried to give you an assessment of the Doctrine Report, in its limitations, its descriptive value and some of its particular achievements in the work of synthesis. It was, however, apparent both to the authors and to the readers of *Doctrine in the Church of England* that the change of climate between 1922, when the Commission began its work, and 1937, when it finished it, was enormous. Temple himself recorded this in the Preface, in some very significant words:

> As I review in thought the result of our fourteen years of labour, I am conscious of a certain transition in our minds, as in the minds of theologians all over the world.... A theology of the Incarnation tends to be a Christocentric metaphysic. A theology of Redemption (though, of course, Redemption had its great place in the former) tends rather to sound the prophetic note; it is more ready to admit that much in this evil world is irrational and strictly unintelligible; and it looks to the coming of the Kingdom as a necessary preliminary to the comprehension of much that now is.... If we began our work again today, its perspectives would be different.

These words were a sign that a theological epoch was near its end.

IV

Let me finish with a final glance at the last few years of William Temple's life. In 1939 there came the catastrophe of the Second

William Temple

World War. In 1942 Temple succeeded to the see of Canterbury and the Primacy of All England: it is doubtful whether a theologian of such original power and genius had done so since S. Anselm. It could hardly be expected that he would continue creative theological work. But still he could guide, and understand: and help thinkers to understand one another. The need for just these gifts was great, for rapid changes in thought were happening, and the mutual reactions of the newer and the older thinkers were sometimes hasty and irritable. In November 1944, William Temple died.

He had come from being a wistful seeker after orthodoxy to being one of its supreme exponents: but always with the motives of relating the faith to contemporary philosophy and of finding in Christ the key to the unity and rationality of the world. Nothing, therefore, in his last years befitted his greatness more than the humility with which he acknowledged that his quest had failed, and that other tasks were superseding it.

Writing in November 1939, Temple describes the changed theological world:

> When the older theologians offer to men fashioned by such influences a Christian map of the world, these rightly refuse to listen. The world of today is one of which no Christian map can be made. It must be changed by Christ into something very unlike itself before a Christian map of it is possible. We used to believe in the sovereignty of the God of love a great deal too lightheartedly. I have much more understanding now than I had in 1906 or thereabouts (when he said it) of Bishop Gore's passionate outburst at a meeting of the Synthetic Society: 'If it were not for the miracles, and supremely the Resurrection, I should see no more reason for supposing that God is revealed in Jesus Christ than that He is revealed in Nero.'

Temple continued:

> There is a new task for theologians today. We cannot come to the men of today saying, 'You will find that all your experience fits together in a harmonious system if you will only look at it in the illumination of the Gospel' . . . our task with this world is not to explain it but to convert it. Its need can be met, not by the discovery of its own immanent principle in signal manifestation

through Jesus Christ, but only by the shattering impact upon its self-sufficiency and arrogance of the Son of God, crucified, risen and ascended, pouring forth that explosive and disruptive energy which is the Holy Ghost. He is the source of fellowship, and all true fellowship comes from him. But in order to fashion true fellowship in such a world as this, and out of such men and women as we are, He must first break up those fellowships with which we have been deluding ourselves. Christ said that the effect of His coming would be to set much at variance. We must expect the movement of His spirit among us to produce sharper divisions as well as deeper unity.

He went on to say that in consequence of this change, the concern of theologians with the theological status of the Church was far greater than it was in 1910 or 1920: there was now 'a new appreciation of the importance of the Church for faith itself'; 'the Church is a part of its own Creed'.

In these ways Temple saw the theological scene to be changing in ways which his generation had not foreseen, but he himself was now prepared for. Looking into the future, he adds:

> We must dig the foundations deeper than we did in pre-war years, or in the inter-war years when we developed our post-war thoughts. And we must be content with less imposing structures. One day theology will take up again its larger and serener task, and offer to a new Christendom its Christian map of life, its Christocentric metaphysic. But that day can barely dawn while any who are now already concerned with theology are still alive.

Twenty years have passed since Temple wrote those words. Has the day of which he spoke begun to dawn?

CHAPTER ELEVEN

EPILOGUE

I

THE sketch of an era of Anglican theology is now ended. Among the hazards in the writing of it, none has been greater than that of describing Anglican thought apart from the story of Christian thought in its wider setting. The task has been possible only because Anglican theology in this era had a certain isolation.

There was indeed the half-conscious influence of wider movements in philosophic and religious thought. Before our era began, the romantic movement had had deep influence on theology in England, as on the Continent. Of the influence of Hegel's philosophy I have spoken in these lectures, though it was in England Hegelianism in a particular Oxford dress. During this era the evolutionary optimism of nineteenth-century liberalism was powerfully felt; and before it ended the reaction from it came with at least some characteristics common to many parts of Christendom.

The conscious influence of continental theologians was, however, small. Harnack influenced the growth of liberalism in our Church, and Schweitzer gave an exciting impulse to the reaction from it. Otto for a time won attention with his *The Idea of the Holy*, and the word 'numinous' passed into our vocabulary. Foreign commentators (Wellhausen, Holtzmann, Loisy, Lagrange) were read in a restricted circle of scholars; and *Formgeschichte* only slowly made its way across the Channel as the work of Dibelius and Bultmann began to be known in the 'thirties. It was in the 'thirties that the sense of isolation lessened. Karl Barth's prophetic impact was felt; but there was—as we saw—little attention to his precise theological teaching. Maritain among the Roman Catholics, Berdyaev among the

Anglican Theology

Eastern Orthodox dispersion in the West, came to be much read. At the same time, two Swedish scholars, Gustav Aulén and Anders Nygren, were often read and quoted. Aulén, in his *Christus Victor*, assisted in the altering of the balance of thought about the Atonement, and Nygren, in his *Agape and Eros*, presented a dichotomy more challenging than convincing. A sounder work on the same subject is John Burnaby's *Amor Dei*. Amid all these influences—and most of them were not until the 'thirties—Anglican theology went its own way.

Scottish and Free Church theology could scarcely fail to affect the Church of England. In the realm of Biblical criticism and exegesis the coming and going was free and mutual. Anglicans recognized the pre-eminence of Scotland and Nonconformity in Old Testament studies: such names as William Robertson Smith, A. B. Davidson, George Adam Smith, John Skinner and A. S. Peake tell their own tale. In dogmatic theology there was less impact upon us, though Dale, Denney and H. R. Mackintosh had many readers. P. T. Forsyth was little known to Anglicans, except his disciple, J. K. Mozley, before his death. This is curious, as he was in his greatest book dealing with those aspects of the Incarnation with which Anglicans had been struggling. John Oman, of Westminster College, Cambridge was a bold and independent thinker, constantly wrestling with the problem of faith and criticism. The anti-sacramental bias in his mind hindered his influence among Anglicans, but his *Grace and Personality* went far in shewing the relation of divine sovereignty and human freedom.

II

If the Anglican theology in our era was separate from that of the Continent, it was also divided by discernible frontiers from the Anglican theology of earlier and later times. It was an era with a beginning and an ending. If the beginning is seen in the grief which *Lux Mundi* caused to Liddon, the ending is seen in the impression of 'datedness' which a reading of *Doctrine in the Church of England* frequently suggests today.

Epilogue

In the perspective of history, however, we can see that this era possessed many permanent characteristics of Anglican theology. Theological history resembles an iceberg in that there is a part of it which is below the surface, and it is the part which gives ballast and continuity. Among the half-conscious influences there is the influence which a Prayer Book inevitably has in a liturgical Church. The *lex orandi* has its quiet and unobtrusive effect upon the *lex credendi*.

Throughout the story which these chapters have told, certain factors of Anglican continuity have seldom been absent.

(1) The Platonist strain had been characteristic of Anglican divinity since the sixteenth century. Visitors from other theological traditions have often noticed it in us, and—what is significant—they have sometimes noticed our own unawareness of it. It has accounted for the tone of classical humanism in Anglican divinity, sometimes at the expense of the Hebraic aspect of our faith. It has kept at bay the Aristotelian scholastic spirit. Within this era it helped to set a limit to the influence of Hegelian idealism. I am thinking specially of such men as C. C. J. Webb and A. E. Taylor, who recalled Anglican thought to the 'philosophia perennis'. The Platonist strain linked our era with the continuing story of Anglicanism. But there was the big difference between Inge, for whom Platonism was a primary medium for theology itself, and Gore and Temple, for whom it was a handmaid with—as between the two of them—somewhat different rôles.

(2) There is the Anglican sensitivity to the significance of spirituality, the life of prayer, for theology. We see this often, from Lancelot Andrewes to William Temple. In the present century the growing interest in the study of religious experience, of the psychology of religion and of mystical phenomena seen in that context, might have led many into subjectivism and shallowness, had not Anglican thought drawn upon the deep stream of Christian spirituality coming from past centuries. During our era there came a revival of interest in the great masters of the spiritual life. It meant much also that not a few Anglicans were learning from the writings of Baron von Hügel

Anglican Continuity

a new sense of man's adoration of his Creator. Nor can the more popular influence of Evelyn Underhill, herself a disciple of von Hügel, be easily belittled. The width and depth of K. E. Kirk's study of many centuries of spirituality in the *Vision of God* shews how Anglicanism can draw upon something larger than itself, to correct and deepen passing tendencies which might become trivial and shallow.

The unity of theology and spirituality owed much to the revival of the monastic vocation. I mention only R. M. Benson, the founder of the Cowley Fathers, whose profound grasp of the Creed was in the context of the life of prayer, and J. N. Figgis of Mirfield, whose writings on the *Gospel and Human Needs* and *Civilization at the Cross Roads* exposed the inner disease of Edwardian culture with the power of one who was monk as well as scholar and prophet.

(3) There is the constant Anglican devotion to Scripture and the Fathers, and some of this appeared in our era with a detachment from the flux of current tendencies. I think, for instance, of H. B. Swete, who succeeded Westcott as Regius Professor of Divinity at Cambridge (1890–1917): textual scholar, exegete, patristic scholar, expounding with precision and with pastoral sympathy the text of Scripture and the doctrines of the faith, training and inspiring younger scholars, including some, like J. M. Creed, whose work was more 'of the times'. None more than Swete represents the continuity of Anglican spirit, to which the enterprises of a particular age owe so much.

(4) There is the constant Anglican care for *Via Media*. This has been seen in different ways. It is seen in the choice of middle ground between strongly entrenched rival camps—like Hooker's middle ground between Rome and Geneva. It is seen in the dislike of pressing aspects of theology with the ruthless logic of a self-contained system. It is seen in the tendency for mediation between schools of thought or religious movements within, or without, our Church. It is seen in the instinct for distinguishing doctrines of lesser and greater import, a bequest of Hooker to the ages which followed him. This care for *Via Media* was

strongly present in divines of our era. It was present in Gore, though it was not his most characteristic gift. It was markedly present in A. C. Headlam, O. C. Quick and Temple himself. It assisted Anglican coherence and continuity.

Thus it was that the Anglicanism of our era, constantly involved with many forces in contemporary thought and culture, was affected—often in the potent realm of the subconscious—by Platonism, by spirituality, by its traditional scholarship and by the care for *Via Media*. These influences made for integrity and for depth at a time when facile and shallow syntheses were all too easy. If these dangers were not avoided, they were at least corrected by influences deeper than contemporary fashions.

III

It has to be asked how the Anglicanism of this era stood in relation to the Reformation theology of the sixteenth century. There was for all typical Anglicans, not least those of the Anglo-Catholic school, no hesitancy on the cardinal convictions of the Reformation: that works cannot earn salvation, that salvation is by grace alone received through faith, that nothing can add to the sole mediatorship of the Cross of Christ, that Holy Scripture is the supreme authority in doctrine. But the most creative Anglicans of our era were little interested in Reformation categories as the media of theological thought, or in Reformation Confessions as the pattern for theological system. They looked far more to Scripture and the Fathers, as the Caroline divines had done before them. In particular, they were less concerned to define, in the sixteenth-century manner, the depth of man's depravity, than to emphasize that man, although fallen, is created in the image of God, after God's likeness.

These Anglicans were, in fact, following the view of the Anglican vocation which finds classic expression in Dean Church's famous essay on 'Lancelot Andrewes' in the volume *Pascal and Other Sermons*. Church insisted that the work of the Anglican Reformation cannot be defined by reference to

Anglican Reformation

the Elizabethan divines alone. In the first phase there was the assertion of the appeal to Scripture and antiquity, and of the claims of the new knowledge. But, amid the controversies of the time, how could the implications of that assertion be grasped with fullness and balance? There were all too many false antitheses, and questions ill-defined. There was the disproportion in theology through the dominance of particular doctrines which controversy made prominent. Hence there had to be a process of adjustment, and of recovery of the grasp of the ancient Catholic Church as the guide to the fullness of the divine gift in Scripture. 'It cannot be sufficiently remembered that in James I's time, and in Charles II's time in 1662, the Reformation was still going on as truly as it was in the days of Edward VI and Elizabeth.' Thus it fell to the Carolines, while maintaining firmly the protest against Roman errors, to move the centre of theology from the controversial subjects of justification, grace and election to the Incarnation of the Word-made-Flesh.

It was such a view of the Anglican Reformation, as Dean Church had expounded it, which became influential in our era. It enabled tasks of synthesis to be done. One instance of such synthesis was the relating of the Logos doctrine to contemporary movements of thought. Another instance was the recovery within the modern Church of England of a fuller realization of the Communion of Saints when once the doctrine could be disengaged from mediaeval error on the one hand and excessive negation on the other. Yet another instance was the recovery of a richer doctrine of Eucharistic Sacrifice, possible only when some false antitheses of sixteenth-century controversy had been abandoned. In this work of recovery and synthesis, modern Anglican divines have continued what the Carolines had begun.

Inevitably, there was during this era a restlessness about the Thirty-Nine Articles. True, since the Clerical Subscription Act of 1865 there had been required of the clergy, not the 'signing' of the Articles, but a comprehensive assent to 'the Thirty-Nine Articles of Religion, the Book of Common Prayer, and the Ordering of Bishops, Priests and Deacons'. One formulary

Epilogue

could be interpreted by the others. True, also, there had come to be widespread in the Church, not indeed a complete acceptance of the exegesis of the Articles given by Newman in *Tract 90*, but a willingness to see in them much ambiguity as articles of peace. Yet feeling grew that the Articles were remote from that formulation of the Catholic Faith which the modern needs of the Church required. That feeling was vigorously voiced by Gore, who described the Articles as 'a theological standard which has ceased to carry either serious obligation or theological enlightenment'.[1] The chief contrary voice was that of Hensley Henson, who urged the necessity of the Articles as giving the historical platform of the Church of England.[2] A *theological* enthusiasm for the Articles was to be seen before the end of our era in Hoskyns' exposition of them as speaking to the times:[3] an enthusiasm born of a new perception of the significance of the Augustinian strain in our tradition. That perception belongs more to the years *after* our era is ended.

IV

One day the history of Anglican theology from 1939 to 1959 will be written. We can here do no more than note briefly and broadly what has been happening, and ask *Quo tendimus?*

There has been a big change in the relation of theology to the world around it and in the nature of theology as its exponents see it. In place of a common stock of friendly philosophical tendencies for theology to exploit and a body of accepted ethical concepts to which theology could be relevant, there is now a lack of unity both in intellectual concepts and in moral standards. There is the intensely technological culture, to which the language of religion means little. In such an environment the isolation of Biblical theology is very plain. The work of the theologian is understood as the exposition of the Bible 'from within'. If it be indeed true that the Gospel is less

---

[1] *The Reconstruction of Belief*, pp. 974-975.
[2] Cf. H. H. Henson, *Bishoprick Papers*, pp. 102-110.
[3] Cf. p. 138 of the present work.

The 'Oecumenical' Spirit

muffled by attempts at synthesis with the culture of an age, it is no less true that its contact with the age is sometimes far to seek.

Within the world of theology, however, the isolation of Anglicanism has grown less. Prophetic teachers from Europe and America drew English minds beyond the writers of their own Church and country. The 'oecumenical' spirit aroused the interest of different confessions in one another. Anglicans found themselves more involved in general theological trends. There was the new valuation of Old Testament theology in relation to the Hebrew cultus. There were the new interests within New Testament study: the Gospels as 'theological documents', typology, theological word-study. There was the revival of study of the Fathers. There was the revival of liturgical study, not least in unexpected regions. There was a new attention to religious language, partly on account of a concern about 'communication', and partly on account of the questions raised by modern linguistic philosophy. None of these energies is uniquely Anglican. In all of them Anglicans have borne a worthy part by their scholarly work.

Within the Anglican Communion a reshaping of schools of thought and parties has been in process. Anglo-Catholicism is a less consciously defined body, and its ideals and methods are more diffused. Liberal Modernism has waned. Conservative Evangelicanism had a revival, partly aided by the craving for authoritarian security in the tempestuous post-war years. Unity has increased by a greater understanding of the oneness of Word and Sacrament in the liturgy, and the sense of the Church with the altar of God as its centre has deepened. So, too, has the conviction of the mission of the laity within the Church.

There is, however, a distinctive witness still to be borne by Anglican theology out of the depths of its own tradition. Biblical theology is in an unsatisfactory state. It cannot be naïvely invoked as the solution for everything. There is here a task that Anglican theology can yet perform, by keeping alive the importance of history in the manner of its great divines of the past, by strenuous attempts to relate Biblical revelation to other categories of thought in the contemporary world, by striving

Epilogue

to integrate dogma with spirituality in the life of prayer, by presenting the Church as the effectual sign of the supernatural in the midst of the natural order. No less is it necessary to avoid imbibing uncritically the assumptions of contemporary oecumenism, and to meet them with something deeper, if less immediately popular, drawn from our appeal to Scripture and antiquity.

In these tasks not a little can be learned from the era to which these chapters have been devoted. Our eyes can be helped to distinguish synthesis which is superficial and synthesis which is surely grounded, arbitrary liberalism and genuine liberality, facile comprehensiveness and true theological coherence. The fifty years of our study have much to shew as to how theology can, and cannot, ally itself to the culture of an age.

There has been in recent years much striving after order and tidiness. But the theological coherence which a Gore or a Temple exhibited came, not from a quest of tidiness, but from a vigorous wrestling with truth for truth's own sake. Without such theological coherence, the Church's moral witness may appear as piecemeal bits of moralizing, and the majestic unity of the Church's faith may be too faintly made visible.

In the weighing of our present theological task, and in trying to fulfil it, we may yet learn from the era which I have attempted to trace 'from Gore to Temple'.

APPENDIX A

THE INFLUENCE OF ALBERT SCHWEITZER

I WAS unable within my lectures to do justice to the influence of Schweitzer. His first book on the Gospels, *Das Messianitäts und Leidengeheimnis* (1901), was not translated into English until 1925, when it appeared with the title *The Mystery of the Kingdom of God* (1925). It was this first book which made the stir on the Continent. Then came *Von Reimarus zu Wrede* (1906) which, in the translation, *The Quest of the Historical Jesus* (1910), made Schweitzer's name a theological household word in England. It was not that many accepted his thesis, but that he brought home in an exciting way that the Gospel contains a mysterious and catastrophic element to which liberalism did no justice. The appeal of Schweitzer's character as medical missionary and musician, as well as scholar, won for him an attention unusual for a foreign theologian.

Schweitzer set forth as the central theme of the mission of Jesus the element which liberalism had put on one side; and the element which liberalism had treated as paramount, the ethical teaching, was given only an 'interim-status' before the early coming of the end. Jesus, according to Schweitzer's thesis, taught the imminence of the end, and the catastrophic coming in of the Kingdom of God. His Messiahship was a secret, and it was *this* secret which Judas betrayed to the priests in Jerusalem. Jesus went to His death in order to hasten the end, and died of a broken heart when He did not see its realization. His ministry was short, quivering, other-worldly, lasting only from seed-time to harvest. The criticism by which Schweitzer established his thesis was arbitrary, relying excessively on certain texts in Matthew (e.g. 10 : 23). The appeal of his thesis was that mystery returned. The real Jesus is strange, bewildering, not a reflection of modern idealism. 'As one unknown and without name He comes to us, as by the shore of the lake He came to those fishermen who knew not who He was.... He commands, and to those who obey He will reveal Himself in that which they will have to do and suffer; and as an unspeakable mystery they will come to find who He is.'

Schweitzer's work was commended almost simultaneously by F. C. Burkitt of Cambridge, who wrote a Preface to *The Quest of the Historical Jesus*, and by W. Sanday of Oxford, who discussed him

Appendix A

enthusiastically in his *The Life of Christ in Recent Research*. 'He keeps much closer to the texts than most critics do. . . . He does not, like so many critics, seek to reduce the Person of Christ to the common measure of humanity, but leaves it at the transcendental heights at which he finds it. . . . By doing so, he is enabled to link on, in an easy and natural way, the eschatology and Christology of the Gospels to the eschatology and Christology of S. Paul and S. John' (pp. 88–89). Encouraged by Burkitt and Sanday, many English students read Schweitzer, and were led to a conviction that the mysterious and catastrophic elements cannot be eliminated from the record of Jesus and that, for all their difficulty, they provide a bridge between Him and apostolic Christianity.

The practical outcome of Schweitzer's influence may be illustrated in the essay on 'The Eschatological Idea in the Gospel' which F. C. Burkitt contributed to *Cambridge Biblical Essays* (1909). Why did the Christian hope survive, and not the Jewish hope?

> The explanation is at least partly to be found in the way that Christianity had been organized for a time of catastrophe rather than for a time of peace—in other words, in immediate expectation of the Kingdom of God and of the calamities which preceded the coming of the Kingdom (p. 207).

> The Gospel is the great protest against the modern view that the really important thing is to be comfortable (p. 209).

> As long as we believe in our hearts that our property, our arts, our institutions, our buildings, our trust-deeds are the most permanent things in the world, so long we are not in sympathy with the Gospel message (p. 211).

> Meanwhile, it is our duty to work while it is day, rather than to 'take thought' where we and our companions are to sleep the night. For Christians the immediate command was to follow Christ, and we read that when the disciples asked Him about the end of the world His first reply was a warning against paying heed to theories about it (p. 212).

The same note was to be struck by E. C. Hoskyns nearly twenty years later in his *Cambridge Sermons*.

> The one fundamental moral problem is what we should still possess if the whole of our world were destroyed to-morrow, and we stood naked before God. The eschatological belief crudely and ruthlessly sweeps away all our little moral busynesses, strips us naked of worldly possessions and worldly entanglements, and asks what survives the catastrophe (p. 37).

Hoskyns, like Burkitt, owed a big debt to Schweitzer.[1]

[1] Cf. J. O. Cobham, 'Hoskyns, the Sunderland Curate', *Church Quarterly Review*, July–September 1957, pp. 290–293.

Appendix A

If, however, Schweitzer's influence put Eschatology in the centre of the theological scene, it was there as itself a problem as well as an answer. If the eschatological teaching of Jesus be genuine, how is it related to the subsequent development of the Church and interpretation of Christ's Person? Gore, a severe critic of Schweitzer, was sceptical as to there being any relation at all. 'It was only in fact by His ceasing to be remembered as historically He was, that He could be serviceable for the generations to come.'[1] Some critics, of whom Inge was one,[2] inferred from the teaching of Jesus concerning the end that He could have had no intention of instituting Church or Sacraments. Others, such as N. P. Williams in *Essays Catholic and Critical*, argued that the predictions of Jesus about the future were partly fulfilled in the Church as the supernatural order wherein they were realized. But in the course of time the view that the eschatological teaching of Jesus should be interpreted 'futuristically' (to use the horrid jargon which theologians have come in recent years to write) has been greatly modified by exegesis interpreting the eschatology as 'realized' already in the presence of Jesus proclaiming the Kingdom and in the Church where the life in Christ is found. This modification of eschatology, made familiar on the Continent by Rudolf Otto's book *Reichgottes und Menschensohn* and by the writings of C. H. Dodd in England, became widely influential, not least in Anglican circles, in the nineteen-thirties. It does not exclude a future and final coming. Living already within the Kingdom which has come, the Christians pray, Thy kingdom come.

It has come to be seen that Schweitzer's error was not to grasp that, because it was Jesus who proclaimed the eschatology, it was transformed from its previous Jewish content by the fact of its association with Himself. Burkitt made this point in his book, *The Earliest Sources for the Life of Jesus* (1911, new edition 1922).

> There is a sense, on the eschatological view, in which it is true to say that Jesus had radically changed the messianic ideal. He had changed it, not by 'spiritualizing' it, but by adding to it. The ideal of King Messiah, coming in glory on the clouds of heaven to judge the world and vindicate the elect of God, he left untouched, but he prefixed to it a prologue. He prefixed to it not a doctrine about Messiah, but the actual course of his own career. We call it his *Ministry*—why? Because his view of the office of the Man who was predestined to be Messiah was that he should 'minister' to the needs of God's people. According to Mark, Jesus went up to Jerusalem to die, to be killed, believing that thereby the Kingdom of God would come. And his great resolve has to be judged in the light of its amazing success (p. 193).

---

[1] *The Reconstruction of Belief*, p. 334.
[2] *Outspoken Essays*, Series I, pp. 227–229.

Appendix A

The ministry and the death were not incidents on the way: they were of the essence of the Kingdom, a very part of the Last Things. Schweitzer's own service of Christ in the heroic vocation of a medical missionary was practical proof that this is so. He came to affirm as much in the new Preface to the third edition (1952) of his *Quest of the Historical Jesus*. 'Jesus introduced into the late-Jewish conception of the Kingdom his strong ethical emphasis on love, making this and the consistent practice of it, the indispensable condition of entrance. By so doing, he charged the idea of the Kingdom of God with ethical forces which transformed it into the reality with which we are familiar' (p. xv). What was originally relegated to the 'interim' is now affirmed to belong to the heart of the matter. It is characteristic of a wheel that it turns.

APPENDIX B

THE FALL AND ORIGINAL SIN IN ANGLICAN THOUGHT

THE abandonment of belief in an historical story of Adam and Eve created a problem in many religious minds, for whom the idea of man as a fallen creature had been bound up with this particular story. It became an immediate task for theology to shew that the Jewish and Christian belief in man's fallen state was independent of the Adam and Eve story, and that it is a belief compatible with the evolution of species. Anglican theologians rose to this task, and in the succeeding years gave much attention to the doctrines of the Fall and Original Sin upon which theories of evolution must needs have considerable bearing.

In the tenth edition of *Lux Mundi*, issued in 1890, Gore provided an Appendix 'On the Christian Doctrine of Sin'. Meeting at once the plea that belief in man's fallen state 'falls to the ground if Genesis is myth and not history', Gore claims that the doctrine 'rests on the strong foundation of the authority of our Lord, accepted and verified by man's moral consciousness'. As to evolution, Gore says: 'The Christian religion represents man as starting in a state of perfection, and gradually degrading. Science, with all the evidence on its side, represents man as starting in a state of savagery and gradually rising'—but 'the historical development of man has not been the development simply as God meant it. It has been tainted through its whole fabric by an element of moral disaster, of human wilfulness.' Gore gives a warning that the idea of man's initial 'perfection' calls for cautious expression, for if the word is permissible it is a perfection *relative* to a stage of development. As to sin, Gore affirms, as unaffected by evolution, the two aspects of sin which history and Christian consciousness make plain, the guilt of each individual man and the antecedent tendency in which all men share. Sin is not a 'substance': it is the misuse of the will. 'Yet each man does not start afresh. He inherits the moral conditions from which his life starts. . . . My sins are only fresh specimens of what has been going on all along.' This essay shows those convictions of Christian consciousness which were to affect the subsequent

Appendix B

theological treatment of the problems, and it also shows that formidable questions remained to be answered.

As to the nature of sin, it was not long before a theory appeared that it was an atavistic survival of animal tendencies in the evolving human species. Thus J. M. Wilson wrote (in words quoted with approval by F. R. Tennant in his *The Origin and Propagation of Sin*, p. 82): 'To the evolutionist sin is not an innovation, but is the survival or misuse of habits and tendencies that were incidental to an early stage of development, whether of the individual or of the race, and were not originally sinful but actually useful. Their sinfulness lies in their anachronism: in their resistance to the evolutionary and divine force that makes for moral development and righteousness.' This theory had some vogue. But it was not difficult to point out that man's worst moral disasters have happened, not by his yielding to animal lusts, but by his wilful misuse of his most refined and advanced mental, and even spiritual, capacities. A more discerning correlation of the facts of evolution and sin was made by S. A. McDowall in a perhaps too little-known work, *Evolution and the Need of Atonement* (1912). McDowall, himself a biologist, shews an analogy between response to environment in the sub-human and the human species. Just as a species which failed to respond to its physical environment did not develop the characteristics needed for survival and deteriorated, so the human species failed to respond to the spiritual environment represented by conscience and the rudiments of moral awareness, and hence morally deteriorated, the aptitude for response becoming blunted. The main line of Anglican theology, without adherence to specific theories, held that, before historical record can begin, moral wilfulness in the human race brought about a moral estrangement from the race's own ideals. This is sin, with its double aspect of inherited tendency and individual responsibility. But 'the Fall' need not be construed as a collapse from a primitive perfection: it is more intelligible as a deviation from the right onward path, such as the diagram of a curve might serve to describe better than a downward line.

As to the definition of sin, traditional theology had distinguished 'actual' sin as the deeds for which an individual is accountable, and 'original' sin as the corporate tendency to sin in the race. In the early years of this century there was much discussion in Anglican circles of the pleas made by F. R. Tennant for the restriction of the term 'sin' to the former: 'moral imperfection for which an agent is in God's sight accountable'.[1] On the other hand, vigorous defence was

---

[1] Cf. F. R. Tennant, *The Origin and Propagation of Sin* (Hulsean Lectures, 1902), *The Doctrines of the Fall and Original Sin* (1903), *The Concept of Sin* (1912).

Appendix B

made of the traditional term.[1] Tennant's view was held to imply too individualistic a conception of sin, whereas the traditional view sees sin as the collective condition of a race alienated from God and bound to confess a common guilt and burden and to seek a redemption, not only of men within society, but of society itself into the corporate new humanity in Christ. Furthermore, those tendencies which are not a man's fault are none the less his responsibility, for he is responsible to put himself in the way of deliverance from them. The vindication of the traditional view is seen eventually in the Report on *Doctrine in the Church of England*.

> What seems to be of practical importance in the conception of Original Sin may be summarized as follows: Man is by nature capable of communion with God, and only through such communion can he become what he is created to be. 'Original Sin' stands for the fact that from a time apparently prior to any responsible act of choice a man is lacking in this communion, and, if left to his own resources and the influence of his natural environment, cannot attain to his destiny as a child of God (p. 64).

This is a correct and uninspiring statement of what Gore taught with passionate conviction in expounding 'Adam' as the symbol both of the guilt of each of us, calling for our conversion, and of the antecedent estrangement of the race, calling for its deliverance into the new humanity of the New Man, Christ.

There were, however, a crop of misunderstandings to be sorted out and eradicated in the history of the doctrine. Original sin, in the broad sense just described, was all too easily confused with the Augustinian doctrine of 'original guilt'. It was necessary to disengage doctrines which had primitive and Catholic authority from doctrines which were purely Augustinian. This task, begun by F. R. Tennant, was completed in the thorough survey by N. P. Williams in his Bampton Lectures for 1924 on *The Doctrines of the Fall and Original Sin*. Williams shews that Catholic authority cannot properly be ascribed to the Augustinian concepts of the original righteousness of Adam in the sense that he had the perfection of a saint, the sharing of the whole race in the *guilt* of Adam's initial sin, the inherent sinfulness of the sex act and the damnation of unbaptised infants. Only very partially accepted in the mediaeval Church, these particular doctrines cannot claim the test of the Vincentian Canon. The Reformers revived some of the Augustinian doctrines in full rigour: yet Williams shews that their presence in the Thirty-Nine Articles is very limited as compared with what the Calvinists would have liked.

---

[1] See especially E. J. Bicknell, *The Christian Idea of Sin and Original Sin in the Light of Modern Knowledge*, 1922.

Appendix B

Williams' work is a salutary analysis, and it serves to shew the strength of the Anglican appeal to Catholic antiquity when pursued with scholarly discrimination.

Why did sin originate? And what is to be said of 'evil' in the created world, apart from man? Christian theology rejects any ultimate dualism. Some Anglican theologians in the period, sensitive to suffering in the animal creation and to disaster in the world such as cannot be laid to the account of human sin, had recourse to the theory of the fall of a 'world-soul' as the origin of evil. Some popularity was gained for this thesis from Canon Peter Green's *The Problem of Evil* (1920), C. W. Formby's *The Unveiling of the Fall* (1923) and the later chapters of the work of N. P. Williams already mentioned; but the utterly mythological character of the idea has led to a decline in the attention given to it. The main trend of theology has been to refrain from speculations about the origin of evil, and to postulate only that rebellious wills (human or angelic or both) are its cause. The possibility of sin is a corollary of freedom. Where sin exists, a painless world would be a world with dim moral possibilities; and, meanwhile, the pain of the world has its rôle in the spiritual education of man, and the grace of God enables the transforming of suffering to redemptive purposes. No more profound, sensitive and practically helpful exposition of these last themes exists than in Temple's *Christus Veritas*.[1] The value of his exposition is drawn from the basic Christian assumption, and does not depend upon the particular philosophy which elsewhere enters the argument of the book.

Elsewhere in *Christus Veritas* Temple argues that the 'fall' may as well be called a 'rise', as man's discovery of the possibilities of wrongdoing was the gate to a hitherto unattainable good. I have discussed in Chapter X (pp. 150–151) Temple's philosophic attempt to shew the place of evil within the rationality of the universe. Anglican theology as a whole did not embrace this line of thought.

On no subject more than that of Sin and the Fall did Anglican theology shew through the years the ability to meet the shocks of criticism, to conserve and reinterpret the essence of traditional belief, to be guided by the fundamental findings of Christian consciousness as well as by the data of science, and to avoid entanglement with passing and superficial syntheses.

[1] See specially *Christus Veritas*, pp. 192–199.

APPENDIX C

THE DOCTRINE OF THE TRINITY IN ANGLICAN THEOLOGY

It is commonly said that modern Anglican theology has been marked by a tendency to emphasize the 'social' aspect of the doctrine of the Trinity, and to present the conception less in terms of one God in three modes of His being than in terms of Three who, in the perfection of infinite love, share in the single essence of Deity. This impression is recorded by D. M. Baillie in his *God was in Christ* (pp. 137-140). In examining this impression and asking how far it calls for qualification, I would try to describe the main lines of Anglican work upon the doctrine in our period.

(1) Throughout Anglican teaching after *Lux Mundi* there is a constant emphasis upon the revelation of the Trinity through history and experience. As to the mode of this revelation, Gore wrote in his Bampton Lectures: 'It is important to notice that there is no moment when Jesus Christ expressly reveals this doctrine. It is overheard rather than heard. It is simply that, in the gradual process of intercourse with Him, His disciples came to recognize Father, Son and Holy Ghost as included in their deepening and enlarging thought of God' (p. 131). Illingworth, who was very conservative in matters of criticism, wrote of the doctrine as if it were verbally revealed by Christ, citing the Baptismal Formula in Matthew 28 as evidence.[1] But the main trend was to appeal, not to any idea that Christ Himself gave teaching about the doctrine, but to the apostolic experience of the Father, the Divine Christ and the Holy Spirit. This line of exposition was worked out very fully by L. Hodgson in his *The Doctrine of the Trinity* (1943). He sees the revelation of the doctrine in events: 'the doctrine of the Trinity is the result of God opening the eyes of men to see the theological significance of those divine acts to which the Bible bears witness' (p. 7). He sees it no less in the nature of the life of sonship which the early Christians experienced, towards the Father, through Christ, in the Spirit (p. 8). Hodgson brilliantly draws out what had been the characteristic Anglican approach for

[1] Illingworth, *The Doctrine of the Trinity*, p. 54.

Appendix C

several decades: God as He was made known in the apostolic history and experience is God as He eternally is.

There is, however, in the discussion of historical origins the difficulty felt by critical minds about the relation of the Holy Spirit to the Risen Christ. Does the New Testament invariably distinguish them? Are we to understand the Spirit to be personal in the sense in which Christ is personal? To the immense discussion of these questions of criticism and interpretation there were two notable Anglican contributions. The first was by K. E. Kirk, writing on 'The Evolution of the Doctrine of the Trinity' in the volume *Essays on the Trinity and the Incarnation* (1928). Kirk here faces the question: allowing that there was in early Christian thought both a binitarian and a trinitarian strain, was the adoption of the latter by the Church due to presuppositions and philosophical influences? His answer was to shew that intellectually a binitarian presupposition was strongly present in Hebraic and in Greek thought, and the victory of the trinitarian position was due to the force of the distinctive Christian experience. There is the other question: in that experience is there a real distinction between Christ and the Holy Spirit? Kirk sees it in the relation of 'communion' (Christ) and the relation of 'possession' (the Spirit), both being distinct though bound together in the Christian's relation to God. 'Man recognizes in the "Son" and in the "Spirit" the respective termini of relations between himself and God, so real that they must be dignified with the title of hypostases' (p. 236).

The other important treatment of this same question is in L. S. Thornton, *The Incarnate Lord* (also 1928—a vintage year in Anglican theology), where Chapter XII is given to 'The Word and the Spirit'. Examining the New Testament evidence, Thornton finds different functions ascribed to Christ and the Spirit in the Christian life, describable respectively as the goal or content of that life and the agent whereby it is built up. 'Both Christ and the Spirit dwell in the Christian soul, but not in the same way. Christ is the indwelling content of the Christian life. He is being "formed" in us. The goal of this process is a conformity of the Christian to the likeness of Christ's character. We are to be conformed to His image . . . S. Paul nowhere says that the Spirit is formed in us, or that we are to be conformed to the image of the Spirit' (p. 323). This distinction applies to the growth of the Christian in grace, and to the building up by the Spirit of the common life of which Christ is the head and the content. Thornton goes on to find a like distinction in the cosmic functions of the Word and the Spirit. The Spirit is at work *within* the created world, moulding within it the material of the new order

Appendix C

when it is redeemed into Christ, who transcends it. This exposition gives considerable place to the Spirit's work within nature; the cosmic function of the Spirit serves and depends upon the cosmic status of the Christ.

In these ways Anglican theologians, setting the doctrine of the Trinity in the ground of history and experience, did not neglect the most difficult questions in the understanding of that history and experience.

(2) In the formulation of the doctrine of the Trinity it is true that Anglican divines favoured the social analogy. There may be two reasons which explain this. One reason is that their usual starting-point has been the Gospels, rather than the exposition of the Godhead in terms of systematic theology. That is a difference between Gore and Hodgson on the one hand, and Aquinas, Calvin and Barth on the other. The Fourth Gospel, in particular, compels the thought that the Son is a 'He' in relation to the Father as a 'He', and the Paraclete is no less a 'He': and this relation in the Son's historic mission is the unveiling in time of the essential being of Deity in eternity, 'the glory which I had with thee before the world began'. For all the immense caution requisite in the application of this language to the One God, the very use of it sets thought about the Trinity in the realm of social analogy.

The other reason is that the concept of 'Personality' loomed large in Anglican thought from the 'nineties. It was an interest derived from idealism. The argument ran thus. Human personality is the most significant phenomenon in the universe, and the key to its interpretation, revealing in turn the divine personality of which it was itself an inadequate image. In its perfection personality is marked, not by solitariness and separateness, but by a threefoldness of existence (intelligence, memory and will) and by a power of social penetration beyond itself. In the Triune God there is the perfection of personality. Such is the line of thought in Illingworth's *Personality Human and Divine*, and, while he uses the psychological analogies of S. Augustine, he finds the social analogy no less inevitable. The most decisive claim for the social analogy is to be found in C. C. J. Webb's *God and Personality* (1918). Webb argued that it is right to speak not of 'the personality of God', but of 'personality in God'. He contended that in the ancient Fathers, when read in the light of their own use of Scripture, the 'hypostases' of the Trinity are akin in meaning to 'persons' in the modern sense, despite the caveats which need to be made.

There were then these antecedent reasons why Anglican theologians found the social analogy congenial. Gore's disposition was

Appendix C

towards it, though he also used the analogies in S. Augustine and believed that the two types of analogy were complementary attempts to express the inexpressible. 'It requires indeed a philosophical microscope to distinguish in final outcome the doctrine of the Cappadocians who began with the Three from the doctrine of Augustine and Aquinas who begin from the One.'[1] There was, however, a certain tendency to use the term 'person' loosely in a way that was rather suggestive of Tritheism, and Gore himself was not immune from that allegation.[2] In responsible teaching reminders were most frequently given that if 'hypostasis' means more than *mode* or *aspect* it means less than *person* in the modern sense. Temple, in *Christus Veritas*, wrote of 'Three Centres of One Consciousness', Thornton, in *Essays Catholic and Critical*, of 'Three Centres of One Activity'. W. R. Matthews, in his *God in Christian Thought and Experience*, bids us learn from both types of analogy.

> If the human personality shews a multiplicity in unity, if further there are three fundamental aspects or functions included within it, then it is not absurd to hold that there is a triune nature of God; and if again the most perfect societies known to us exhibit a multiplicity in unity, and if this unity becomes the more complete as the society becomes more perfect, there is nothing contrary to reason in supposing the divine Nature to exhibit these characteristics in the most complete manner.... It seems to me that ... the two analogies really converge (pp. 192–193).

Furthermore, it must not be forgotten that, in the midst of an era said to be marked by a social doctrine of the Trinity, Anglican divinity contains one of the most forceful statements ever made of the Divine Unity. It is in R. C. Moberly's *Atonement and Personality*. Complaining that there is too often 'among those who wish to make a point of being orthodox a great deal of practical tritheism', Moberly says

> Supposing for a moment that this 'is not' lies at the heart of the distinction of one human person from another; in any case 'is not' is not the heart of the distinction of the Three Persons of Deity. Thus to say that the Father is not the Son, and that the Son is not the Spirit, whatever element there may be in it of truth—and of course there is truth in it—is yet to say, to our apprehensions, too much. For each is God, the one God, and all are inseparable (p. 167).

To the many analogies used in Trinitarian thought Moberly adds one more of his own. 'There is the man as he really is in himself,

---

[1] *The Reconstruction of Belief*, p. 544.
[2] Cf. C. E. Raven, *Jesus and the Gospel of Love*, p. 285.

Appendix C

invisible, indeed and inaccessible—and yet, directly, the fountain, origin and cause of everything that can be called in any sense himself. Secondly, there is himself as projected into conditions of visibleness—the overt expression or utterance of himself. . . . And thirdly, there is the reply of what we call external nature to him—his operation or effect.' (p. 174). This highly original analogy is very near to the process of New Testament revelation. As J. Burnaby has recently pointed out, it anticipates the treatment by Karl Barth,[1] who writes in total unawareness that there is such a thing as Anglican theology.

(3) Recurring in the Anglican divines of the period is a conviction of the importance of the doctrine of the Trinity for the relation between God as absolute Creator and the created world in its dependence upon Him. This is put baldly by Thornton thus:

> In a Unitarian conception of God, where there is no subject-object relation within the Godhead, the idea of creation inevitably comes to mean that the world is the necessary object of divine activity. The world thus takes the place of the Eternal Son, and God is subjected to external necessity. If, however, there are hypostatic distinctions within the Godhead, we can find in God the possibility of creative action without introducing such necessity.[2]

'It alone enables us to think of God as in Himself "the living God" apart from and independently of creation', wrote Gore.[3] The recurrence of this thought shews the concern of theologians, who were dwelling much upon the manifestation of God in nature, to avoid suggestions that God requires nature for His own fulfilment or perfection. No, it is upon God, perfect in Himself in the fullness of the eternal love of Father, Son and Spirit, that the universe utterly depends. It without Him is nothing: He without it is God. He creates and sustains the world in the overflowing of His own perfection. The dogma of the Trinity thus assists man's understanding of the world and of the meaning of his adoration of his Maker.

Thus, throughout the half century under review, Anglican theologians were able to serve the interpretation of the doctrine of the Trinity—with a primary concern for history and experience, a willingness to face the critical questions therein involved, a respect for the ancient terminology, a hospitality to current discussions of

---

[1] Cf. Karl Barth, *Church Dogmatics*, I, pp. 339–383, and the comment by J. Burnaby, *The Belief of Christendom*, p. 209.
[2] *Essays Catholic and Critical*, pp. 145–146.
[3] *The Reconstruction of Belief*, p. 545.

Appendix C

personality and a grasp of the creature–creator relation in its demands upon thought and in its expression in worship. The dogma of the Blessed Trinity speaks of the Christian life, both as sonship and fellowship with the Father, through the Son, in the Spirit, and as adoration of the Triune Name of One God, indivisibly Creator, Redeemer, Sanctifier, to Whom be glory for ever.

APPENDIX D

GORE AND RASHDALL ON THE DOCTRINE OF THE TRINITY

IN Chapter V I described the controversy at the time of the Girton Conference in 1921, when Gore and others criticized the view of the Incarnation taught by Rashdall and Bethune-Baker, on the ground that it seemed to obscure the distinction between Godhead and Manhood, Creator and creature. It would be unfair to history not to notice also the counter-criticism made by Rashdall of Gore in respect of his language about the Persons of the Trinity.

Gore had stated the issue, as he saw it, in a public speech in Birmingham which was widely and fully reported. His biographer describes it thus:

> He distinguished strongly between the conception of God revealed by the Hebrew prophets and 'the idea which has haunted philosophers of almost every generation, what is commonly called the higher pantheism, according to which God and Man are of one substance'. The latter view issued historically in the doctrine known as Adoptionism, according to which Christ's personal existence began with His human birth, and He was divine only in the sense that the divine spirit was united to Him or bestowed upon Him in an exceptional degree. This theory had been considered quite deliberately by the Church, and as deliberately rejected. But he felt no doubt that it was the view maintained by Dr. Rashdall.[1]

Rashdall made a spirited reply in three articles in *The Modern Churchman* entitled 'Some Plain Words to Bishop Gore'.[2] In the first he quoted Gore's words, 'I cannot think that Dr. Rashdall holds that the person who appeared as Jesus Christ was really an Eternal Person in the Blessed Trinity, who at a certain date took flesh and became Man remaining always the same.' Rashdall asks what is meant by 'person', and says that Gore assumes it means 'person' in the modern sense. On the contrary, the ancient words *hypostasis* and *persona* did not carry that meaning. 'The Son' meant for S. Athanasius not a personality distinct from the Father, but the wisdom or mind of the Father. Still more was this so with S. Augustine and S. Thomas

[1] L. Prestige, *The Life of Charles Gore*, pp. 455-456.
[2] *The Modern Churchman*, December 1921; April 1922; July 1922.

Appendix D

Aquinas. The latter held that the distinction between Father, Son and Spirit was the distinction between Power, Wisdom and Love in the same mind. 'It is not necessary to think of the Word before the Incarnation as a mind or consciousness distinct from that of the Father. I agree that this is really the point at issue between Bishop Gore and myself; but once more, to question the position of Bishop Gore is not to deny the Divinity of Christ.' Rashdall makes the further plea that Gore's doctrine of Kenosis is incompatible with the identity, or at least the immutability of the Divine Word.

Rashdall's rejoinder did not meet the biggest issue of all, which is irrespective of the interpretation of the word 'person', namely the relation of Godhead and Manhood. But it made a skilful thrust at one of Gore's weak points: his tendency to use the word 'person' unguardedly. But was Rashdall right in his understanding of the Trinitarian doctrine of Athanasius, Augustine and Thomas Aquinas? Or, put it differently, must anything resembling the analogy of 'person' in the modern sense be extruded from the doctrine?

Unfortunately, Gore never made a full reply, though he took occasion to deal with the value and the limitations of both types of analogy in his *Belief in Christ*, 1922.[1] The answer to Rashdall was given first with any fullness in a note on 'The Trinitarian Doctrine of Augustine and Aquinas' by E. J. Bicknell in *Essays Catholic and Critical*. He sets forth evidence suggesting that Rashdall had oversimplified the teaching both of Augustine and of Aquinas. In Augustine there are passages on the *relation* between the persons akin to the descriptions in Scripture (*De Trinitate*, IV, 30, V. 6). The analogies from a single mind are balanced by that of the one who loves and the one who is loved (VIII, 14). He insists on the inadequacy of illustrations borrowed from the functioning of a single self (XV, 12, 45). Bicknell makes the interesting comment, 'Augustine gets more modalistic, the further he gets away from scripture.' As to Aquinas, the dominant analogy is that of functions within a single human mind. Yet there is evidence in his writings of the inadequacy of the single human mind to furnish a complete illustration of the threefold process of the divine life (cf. *Summa Theologica*, I, xxxi, 2; xxxiii, 2; xxxix, 4). The impression is left from this evidence that Rashdall had pressed what is admittedly the central argument of both Augustine and Aquinas with ruthless logic, and neglected to see the evidence in the broadest way.

The case was put later in a similar way by L. Hodgson in his *The Doctrine of the Trinity* (pp. 158–165). To the evidence assembled by Bicknell he adds further evidence to show that, where they are

---
[1] See *The Reconstruction of Belief*, pp. 537–544.

Appendix D

nearest to Modalism, Augustine and Aquinas are constrained by the logic of the philosophical premises which they are using, but that the religion in which they believe, coming down to them from Scripture, contains a Trinitarianism to which the analogy of the single mind is inadequate.

> Is it conceivable [asks Hodgson] that the author of the eucharistic hymn, *Adoro te devote*, should ever have thought the words 'the Eternal Son' to mean no more than that God is wise as well as being powerful and loving? The Trinity of God's self-revelation is no impersonal system of relations between hypostases in an essence; it is the living, loving communion of Father, Son and Spirit into which we are adopted in Christ. Neither in St. Augustine nor in St. Thomas can their logical apparatus conceal the fact that this is the living reality in which they believe, about which they are trying to think and write.

The reader should test the evidence by which Bicknell and Hodgson respectively reach their conclusions before he accepts uncritically the sweeping remark which Dr. Pittenger has recently allowed himself to make: 'The annihilation which Bishop Gore suffered at the hands of Hastings Rashdall'.[1] The evidence suggests that this judgment is far from true.

[1] *Anglican Theological Review*, October 1955, XXVII, 4, p. 264.

INDEX OF SUBJECTS

Apostolic Succession, 111–119, 124–127, 137
Atonement, 4, 9, 23, 44–59, 76, 103, 159–161
Authority, 5–6, 97–101, 104–106, 109

Bible, 5–6, 95–101, 129–145, 163, 165, 169

Church, 5–6, 7, 97–101, 111–128, 143–144, 161
Creation, 16–18, 23, 24–26, 59
Creeds, 21–22, 77–91

Doctrine in the Church of England, 90–91, 156–159

Eschatology, 9, 142–143, 171–174
Eucharist, 10, 51–53, 104, 115, 157–159
Evangelicalism, 53–55, 141, 155–156
Evolution, 3–5, 17, 24–26, 69, 175–177
Experience, religious, 63–66, 95–97, 104–106

Fathers, the ancient, 3, 5, 21–23, 31–32, 97–101, 116–119, 165, 167
Foundations, 23, 80, 148

Girton Conference, 1921, 69–73, 86–87

Holy Spirit, 5–6, 26, 47, 97–98

Idealism, or Hegelianism, 9–10, 24–25, 68–69, 148–151
Immanence, 3–5, 24–26, 68–69, 89

Justification, 55–56, 139, 166

Liberal Protestantism, 53–55, 61–62, 134
Liturgy, 50, 144, 164, 169

Miracle, 19–21, 74–76, 77–83, 88–91, 95–97
Modernism, Catholic, 63–66, 101
Modernism, English, 60–76, 86–87, 90–91, 157
Monasticism, 165

Oecumenical Movement, 124, 144, 154, 169–170

Platonism, 66, 94, 164

Reunion, 119–128, 156
Revelation, 8, 16–18, 95–101, 141–142, 151–153

Sacrifice, 44–47, 50–53, 56–57, 104, 157–158
Sin and the Fall, 17–18, 21, 23–24, 45, 49–50, 76, 175–178
Sociology, 14–15, 154–155
Spirituality, 46, 107, 165
Suffering, 44–45, 58–59, 178

Thirty-Nine Articles, 138–139, 167–168

Validity, 118, 123–126

INDEX OF NAMES

Andrewes, Lancelot, 43, 164, 166
Aulen, G., 56, 163

Baillie, D. M., 42, 179
Barth, Karl, 137, 141–142, 153, 162, 181, 183
Beare, F. W., 42
Benson, R. M., 165
Berdyaev, N., 162
Bethune-Baker, J. F., 25, 66, 69–72, 86, 90, 185
Bicknell, E. J., 103, 177, 186
Bright, W., 35, 36, 51
Brilioth, Y., 104
Brunner, E., 142
Bultmann, R., 162, 171–172, 173
Burkitt, F. C., 130, 171, 172, 173
Burnaby, J., 163, 183

Caird, E., 25, 148
Campbell, McLeod, 47
Campbell, R. J., 25
Chase, F. H., 81
Church, R. W., 166–167
Cobham, J. O., 132, 172
Creed, J. M., 40–42, 165

Dale, R. W., 46, 53, 55, 163
Davey, F. N., 134, 139
Davies, J. Conway, 93
D'Arcy, C. F., 58
Davidson, Randall, 12, 81–83, 84–85, 88–89, 156
Denney, J., 53, 55, 163
Dibelius, M., 162
Dodd, C. H., 127, 141, 143, 173
Dörner, I. A., 33

Fairbairn, A. M., 33
Fairweather, E. R., 42

Fawkes, A., 86–87
Figgis, J. N., 165
Foakes-Jackson, F. J., 70, 86–87
Formby, C. W., 178
Forsyth, P. T., 38–40, 41, 53, 55, 116, 163

Gardner, P., 66
Glazebrook, M. G., 68, 74
Glover, T. R., 62
Gore, Charles, life and character, 2, 13–14, 78, 92–94; on the Bible, 5–6, 97–101; social teaching, 14–15; on the Incarnation, 16–24; on dogmatic formulae, 21–23; on Creeds, 77–80; on kenosis, 6, 33–35; on atonement, 23, 49–50; on the Eucharist, 10, 51–52; on modernism, 68, 73, 75, 78–85; on Reconstruction of Belief, 95–101; on the Church, 97–101, 111–116, 127–128; contrasted with Temple, 146–147; on Schweitzer, 173; on Sin and the fall, 175; on the Trinity, 183, 185–187
Goudge, H. L., 70
Green, Peter, 178
Green, T. H., 2, 8–10, 13

Hamilton, H. F., 130
Hamilton-Thompson, A., 104
Harnack, A. von, 27, 61, 63, 64, 132, 162
Headlam, A. C., 117–118, 122, 166
Headlam, Stewart, 2
Hebert, A. G., 144
Henson, H. H., 78, 83–87, 89, 121, 168
Hicks, F. C. N., 52
Hodgson, L., 179–180, 181, 186–187

Index of Names

Holland, H. S., 2, 6, 10, 12–15, 44–46, 49, 52, 80, 139, 140
Hooker, R., 75, 165
Hort, F. J. A., 1, 2, 3, 7, 26
Hoskyns, E. C., 103, 107, 131–140, 145, 168, 172

Illingworth, J. R., 4–5, 11, 20, 24, 179, 181
Inge, W. R., 65, 66–67, 86, 139, 164, 173
Iremonger, W., 89

Jowett, B., 60

Kelly, Fr. H. H., 142
Kidd, B. J., 36
Kirk, K. E., 55, 103, 107–108, 165, 180
Knox, W. L., 105, 155

Lacey, T. A., 65, 122, 155
Lake, K., 70, 86–87, 96
Liddon, H. P., 2, 7–8, 33, 35, 43, 163
Lightfoot, J. B., 1, 116–117, 139
Lloyd-Morgan, C., 26
Lock, W., 7
Loisy, A., 63–65, 139
Lubac, H. de, 127
Lyttleton, A., 7

Mackintosh, H. R., 22–23, 38, 163
Major, H. D. A., 67, 73, 74
Maritain, J., 162
Mascall, E. L., 10, 35, 42
Matthews, W. R., 147, 182
Maurice, F. D., 2, 45, 112, 122, 142
McDowall, S. A., 176
Mersch, E., 127
Milner-White, E., 103
Moberly, R. C., 6, 11, 12, 13, 46–49, 50–53, 55, 112, 182–183
Moore, Aubrey, 3, 4, 6, 11
Moule, Handley C. G., 53
Mozley, J. B., 19
Mozley, J. K., 55, 103, 163

Newman, J. H., 99, 111, 168
Niebuhr, R., 153
Nygren, A., 163

Oman, J., 54, 55, 163
Ottley, R. L., 7, 10, 12
Otto, R., 162, 173

Paget, F., 2, 7, 12, 88–89
Pattison, Pringle, 25
Pittenger, W. N., 72, 81, 187
Pusey, E. B., 2, 43

Quick, O. C., 41–42, 56–57, 86, 107, 123–124, 125, 166
Ramsey, A. M., 26, 124, 127
Rashdall, H., 40, 54–55, 67–70, 86, 90, 185–187
Raven, C. E., 25–26, 70, 182
Rawlinson, A. E. J., 65, 80, 105, 107
Reckitt, M. B., 154
Relton, H. M., 38
Richardson, R. D., 74
Ritschl, A., 27, 61, 152
Robinson, J. Armitage, 81, 88, 130

Sanday, W., 35, 68, 79–80, 84, 130, 139, 171–172
Schweitzer, A., 27, 61, 63, 162, 171–174
Selwyn, E. G., 75, 76, 101–103, 106
Shebbeare, C. J., 141
Spens, W., 52, 65, 102, 104
Stanley, A. P., 60
Stanton, V. H., 130, 139
Stone, Darwell, 8, 9, 72, 84–85, 118
Storr, V. F., 156
Streeter, B. H., 58, 62, 68, 80, 130
Stubbs, William, 8
Studdert-Kennedy, G. A., 58
Swete, H. B., 51, 118, 130, 165

Talbot, E. K., 153
Talbot, E. S., 2, 6, 12, 80
Taylor, A. E., 80, 97, 103, 108–109, 164

Index of Names

Taylor, Jeremy, 51, 115
Temple, William, life and character, vii, viii, 146–147, 153, 160–161; on the Incarnation, 24–26, 148–149; on the kenosis, 41–42, 146; on the Cross, 56; on suffering in God, 58–59; on subscription, 88–91; on the Church, 124–128; contrasted with Gore, 146–147; his Christian philosophy, 148–151; on creation, 150; on evil, 150–151, 178; on Revelation, 151–153; social teaching, 153–155; on doctrinal unity, 156–159; on the change of theological climate, 159–161
Tennant, F. R., 74, 176–177
Thomasius, 32
Thompson, J. M., 80–81

Thornton, L. S., 24, 25, 26, 74, 103, 107, 127, 143, 180, 182, 183
Turner, C. H., 114, 118, 130
Tyrrell, G., 63–64, 65, 105

Underhill, E., 165

Vidler, A. R., 73–74
von Hügel, F., 59, 64, 164–165

Webb, C. C. J., 9, 10, 164, 181
Wesley, C., 33, 51
Westcott, B. F., 1, 2, 3, 9, 14, 23, 51, 140
Weston, F., 36–38, 40
Whitehead, A. N., 24, 74
Williams, N. P., 103–104, 107, 122, 173, 177–178
Wilson, J. M., 176